No one can remake the past, but mankind has found that historical accounts need to be re-examined periodically.

The NEW INSIGHTS IN HISTORY series provides a contemporary point of view. Each author undertakes an innovative, original reappraisal of a particular segment of history, employing the most recent scholarship and methods to stimulate the study of the past.

L. JAY OLIVA, author of this volume in the New Insights in History series, is Associate Professor of History, New York University. He is also the author of *Misalliance: A Study of French Policy in Russia During the Seven Years War* and editor of *Russia and the West from Peter to Khrushchev*. His many articles on Russian history have appeared in numerous professional publications.

❈

Russia
in the Era of
Peter the Great

❈

L. Jay Oliva, *1933 —*

Prentice-Hall, Inc. A SPECTRUM BOOK *Englewood Cliffs, N.J.*

To Mary Ellen, Jay, and Edward

PRENTICE-HALL INTERNATIONAL, INC. (*London*)
PRENTICE-HALL OF AUSTRALIA, PTY. LTD. (*Sydney*)
PRENTICE-HALL OF CANADA, LTD. (*Toronto*)
PRENTICE-HALL OF INDIA PRIVATE LIMITED (*New Delhi*)
PRENTICE-HALL OF JAPAN, INC. (*Tokyo*)

Preface

This study is intended to introduce students and general readers to Petrine Russia before they are confronted with the contemporary systems which have made so much use of it. This work does not emphasize or insist upon the role of Peter in causing the Russian Revolutions; it does not focus on the role of Peter in shaping or prefiguring the Soviet system; nor does it pretend to demonstrate any nineteenth- or twentieth-century economic theories. All of these perspectives may be eminently worthy of consideration, but this work assumes that one ought to begin by understanding Petrine Russia in its heritage and in its eighteenth-century European environment, an environment in which national identities were being incarnated in state structures, traditional economic and social patterns were significantly altered, and the variety of European traditions and systems were intermingling and feeding one another in substantial ways. Thus armed with a "horizontal" perspective on Petrine Russia, the reader will be in a far better position to judge for himself the validity and the value of the ways in which the Petrine era is utilized to explain the present and foretell the future.

I am indebted to the students who have shared my interest in Petrine Russia; I would like especially to recognize Professor Richard Warner of Mary Washington College for his published article on the Kozhukovo maneuvers, Professor Raymond Mohl of the University of Indiana at Gary for his published article on the colonial image of Peter the Great, and Professor Peter Petschauer of Appalachian State University for his work on Leibnitz. I also thank Professor Daniel Quilty and the members of his department for their hospitality during my leave. The manuscript was prepared by Mrs. Harold B. McNally, whose efficiency and constant good humor contributed so much to my peace of mind. Finally, I praise my wife for bearing the presence of a continually preoccupied husband in her household.

L. Jay Oliva

Sparkill, N. Y.
September 23, 1968

Contents

Introduction

Human nature being circumscribed at least by the limits of time, there are three basic perspectives, each admittedly available in a variety of ideological permutations, from which a historian can view any problem—from the past, the present, or the future. Each of these perspectives has its peculiar advantages and disadvantages. We are speaking here not of historical schools of interpretation but of the way in which any historian of any school will proceed practically. The historian, like Archimedes, must choose some place to stand to wield his interpretive lever even if the burden he intends to lift is not nearly as weighty as the Greek's world.

The view from the past places the historian somewhere behind his problem, from which vantage he applies his tools to the examination of that problem to determine how the past has shaped and directed it. This view inevitably involves the historian in the question of leadership and creativity in history; investigation of the background of any problem reveals forces at work which seem to guarantee its direction and therefore to diminish the role of leadership by demonstrating the overwhelming pressures of roots and precedents. Modern historians by the score and from a variety of "schools" have made their careers by finding the roots of what were once considered "revolutionary" eras deeper and deeper in the past. I have not looked recently into the affairs of my colleagues in American history, but I would guess that the "New Deal" has been posited in its origins to a period well before the administration of Herbert Hoover; I vaguely recall a rather respected work which seemed to place it in the days of Andrew Jackson! The European "Renaissance" has ceased to move into the past by decades and now gallops by centuries. And I read recently in a *New York Times* book review that the "Cold War" dated at least from the Spanish-American War.

The era of Peter the Great can, indeed must, be viewed from its past. Peter was the heir of the "Time of Troubles" and of the Romanov recovery of absolutism and territories, and one needs to stand in the seventeenth century and look forward to the Petrine era to see just how mightily the past shaped Petrine alternatives. Such an approach to a problem—by way of the past—is prone to some form of determinism, for the search after "first causes" becomes interminable, seeking ever backward for the human key to development and forcing scholars in frustration to designate some abstraction as the driving force of history. But the view from the past need not necessarily discredit leadership nor predestine success or failure. One view might be stated simply: that a successful leader is one who penetrates by intellect or by instinct the forces at work in his environment and bends them to his needs. Failures of leadership can be traced to ignorance of, or scorn of, or innate insensibility to the weight of history. It may be that such a view helps to define some forms of historical motion: "revolutions" may be the rapid release of momentous and long frustrated forces at work in a society; "reactions" may well be attempts to prevent such release; "reforms" might be viewed as attempts to harness and direct such forces in prescribed directions; and attempts to manufacture such forces where they do not exist usually end in history books as perplexing, sometimes courageous, and always tragic, failures.

Peter can lay claim to substantial leadership. For all the confusion and emergency character of his reign, Peter displayed an intuitive grasp of his heritage, a monarch's sense of his place in his dynasty, and he employed the developments of the seventeenth century to refashion the absolute state as an instrument to resolve the two most pressing problems of his heritage: the security of his homeland against the neighboring states which threatened it, and the internal order of his realm, which had been seeded with chaos and anarchy. It is well to remember that leadership in these terms has little to do with "goodness" or "badness" but with the accomplishment of chosen ends. One may document the skill with which "leaders" pursue their goals without for a moment wishing to accompany them.

Then there is the "horizontal" view, the contemporary view of a historical problem from the plane of its own times. In assuming such a view an historian makes no pretense at purging himself of subsequent historical lessons, but simply prefers to center his attention on the problem within its own environment. This view usually thrives on the interrelationships of particular historical problems with similar problems in close chronological and geographical proximity. This approach tends to satisfy historians of many schools far more than it does political scientists, for it pleases their sense of scholarship to avoid overt and direct service to their own times, and at the same time enables them to deal in generalizations without which their work seems flat, stale and unprofitable. Here the generalizations concern problems for which time, tradition, and geography set clear limits. One can, as we have seen, compare a historical problem with its past and make judgments. Here we compare the historical problem with its neighbors in time, and in the process make judgments about its peculiarity or its universality and in the process discover that it is not only the past with which leadership must deal but with the commingling of many presents. Every problem has not only a past but a milieu, an environment within which it lives. As a matter of fact, a problem exists within concentric circles of environment, as a family lives in a home within a neighborhood, and the neighborhood within a city, and so on outward to the global milieu. The most important environment of Petrine Russia was early eighteenth-century Europe; Peter's Russia was shaped not only by its past, but was interacting with the forces of the neighborhood around it—that neighborhood of absolute monarchs and secular states riding the crest of a rising tide of "modernity."

Finally, there is the view from the future. This obviously does not mean history written after the problem, which is the condition of all history, but history written from the perspective of how the problem has shaped the future or how the problem enlightens us about our own times. The motto over the National Archives proclaims in unconscious egocentricity which perfectly suits each new age that "the past is prologue." The past can thus be viewed as an explanation of how we got to be "wonderful us," or, depending upon your view of your own age, "despicable us" or "confused us."

Some political scientists and historians bored with academe are especially enamored of this perspective and have a prosperous time in government service ministering to it. We can hardly blame the citizenry (which, contrary to the view of Aristotle, seems far more practical than speculative in its nature) for asking historians what they have done for society lately. There is nothing inherently wrong in examining a historical problem by comparing it with the historian's own present or in confronting your own age and testing your hypotheses about it on past problems, as long as it is recognized that, of the three basic approaches, this one is the most dangerous and potentially the most misleading. Historians bent upon this tack should steep themselves in the other perspectives as well. This view is dangerous because it often causes a confusion of historical focus, in which the scholar seems uncertain whether he is examining his present or the past. It is dangerous, too, because the test of historical value can easily become survival, with other developments blithely "deposited in the rubbish heap of history," to use Trotsky's comment on the tragic Mensheviks. But the most spectacular danger of the "futurist" approach is the tendency to impose modern systems on past problems in order to demonstrate their relevance to current needs, with the same jarring sense of anachronism as when that sixteenth-century clock chimes the hour in Shakespeare's *Julius Caesar*. It is not only dangerous for the historian to take his insights into present problems and impress them upon the past because it distorts the past, but also because it is self-defeating of "futurist" purposes: how can we accurately plumb the forces at work around us if we have seriously misunderstood their development? As a matter of fact, such procedures tend to be self-fulfilling and self-reinforcing; we apply a modern insight to a past era, and then use this evidence of the past to justify in turn the modern principle. "Futurists" have gotten themselves and their times in some serious straits by misreading the past in their own image.

Peter has suffered rather badly at the hands of "futurists" in many generations. The historians working in the revolutionary period of the late eighteenth and early nineteenth centuries, either happy or unhappy with their times, heaped praise or blame upon Peter as a "Tsar Revolutionary" when such a view ignored his horizontal kinship with the foremost European fashioners of the "old regimes." Slavophiles and Westerners of Russia's nineteenth century, suffering through their own crisis of national identity, reflected their arguments back upon Peter and condemned or exalted him as the destroyer or creator of Russian civilization, when either view ignored the obvious directions of his Muscovite inheritance. Soviet historians, depending upon the political complexion of their times, reflected back upon Peter the image of "feudal tool" or "bourgeois tool" or "Stalinist." Western

European and American historians have been just as busy: the concept of "underdeveloped society," so useful in our day, has been
heaved into the Petrine past to paint Peter as the first of a long line
of defensive reformers peculiar to the Russian system and culminating
in Stalin; others, "Cold War" warriors among them, finding in the "iron
curtain" a proof of the natural division between Russia and "western
civilization," reflected that view into Peter's reign and, lo and behold,
found it so. Many of these same analysts, viewing Soviet economic
and military growth as simply technical thievery from the ingenious
"west" have evaluated the achievements of Peter in this light and
thus helped to confirm their original judgment.

Peter can certainly and legitimately be viewed from the perspective
of his contributions to the formation of contemporary society, and
theories abstracted from present events may sometimes enlighten our
understanding of the Petrine age. But one wonders if the diagnos-
ticians of the Cold War, the servants of the dialectic, the analysts of
totalitarian systems, the propagandists for or against Communist ex-
pansionism, or the theoreticians of modern economic growth, have
really contributed much except a new chapter on historiography to
our understanding of Petrine Russia. Their focus on Petrine Russia
has been fuzzy and brief, staying only long enough to harness it to
some modern cause; most of their systems seem as appropriate to
Peter's age as sports cars in the streets of eighteenth-century Petersburg.

There is obviously a little of all three perspectives in the following
pages, although the author intended to pursue only the first two. A
predominantly "horizontal" consideration, the Muscovite past bearing
upon Petrine leadership within the environment of eighteenth-century Europe, seems most useful for an introductory work on the
Petrine Era. The motto here is that he serves the present best who
avoids as well as he can imposing its passions on the past. One may
miss an insight in the process but one will also avoid an immense
amount of nonsense. At the same time it is absolutely certain that an
examination of the era of Peter within the larger frame of the emerging forces of eighteenth-century Europe will serve our understanding
of the present! It is my own conviction, not pressed here, that much
of what we celebrate and bemoan about our "modern" world was
shaped in the eighteenth century, in that most turbulent, most ebul-
lient, most frustrating, and most active of eras, and that Peter is not

least among those monarchs and princes whose political aspirations and military adventures forged the lineaments of the modern world. But, then, some work ought to be left to the energetic reader; let the discovery of such contributions be his task. Every reader living and acting in this complex world must in the end be his own "futurist."

�֍ 1 �֍

Movement in Muscovy

Peter the Great, in delineating the areas of his reforms and in choosing the techniques to accomplish them, strode firmly in the footsteps of his ancestors. Historians have argued the role of Peter's heritage largely from the perspective of the problems of their own age. Most of the historians of the late eighteenth and early nineteenth centuries were prone to see in Peter a great revolutionary, who overthrew and wiped out traditional values and instituted programs wholly original. Some historians, disgusted with their own era of revolutions, viewed such a "revolutionary" Tsar with loathing, believing that he cut down the natural growth of society and implanted artificial shoots in alien soil and thus did irreparable damage to Russia. Other historians more sympathetic to their own revolutions were prone to accept a "revolutionary" Tsar as a necessity, who broke through encrusted superstitions and obstinate obscurantism to force progress and enlightenment upon his people. It is now clear that, for good or evil, Peter was no "tsar-revolutionary" but rather a "tsar-reformer" who built upon the traditions and developments of the Muscovite past. It is also clear that Peter chose some traditions over others, some developments at the expense of others, and that his work was so infused with the dynamism of his towering personality that few of his contemporaries, unaccustomed by the values of their age to look for historical precedents, could see behind him. All this says only that Peter must be viewed from the Russian past. The past is a powerful influence, and men, especially men like Peter whose will is far stronger than their vision, use and direct the past to their purposes. Thus, in aspiring to understand the work of Peter the reasons for its permanence, we must begin by understanding his Muscovite inheritance.

It was a popular and a historical view that Muscovy before 1682 was dark and stagnant, that beneath the fearsome winters deep in the forests on the northern reaches of the Volga, Muscovy wallowed in barbarism, superstition, cruelty and violence. Western European visitors and commentators, fresh from their own varieties of seventeenth-century squalor, described Muscovy as exotic and surely not "European," scarcely willing to believe that the crudity called Orthodoxy deserved to be labeled Christianity. The visitor Olearius of Holstein wrote in 1643 that "if a man considers the natures and manners of life of the Muscovites, he will be forced to avow that there cannot be anything more barbarous than that people." Such a view of the Muscovite past, fostered especially by Muscovy's enemies and encouraged by the fastidious French, fit well into the popular "enlightenment" theory that only with Peter the Great had the curtain of barbarism and ignorance been pierced, only with the introduction of "western" ideas and ideals had Muscovy been called by force into the company of civilized societies and its historical dialectic put into motion. Such a view is dramatically appealing and still popularly widespread, but it is untrue. Muscovy was most certainly in movement when Peter came to direct its destiny and the forms and the directions of that movement certainly shaped the pattern of the Petrine reforms.

Muscovy in the seventeenth century was in territorial movement. Across Europe the primary business of states was the "stabilization" of frontiers, and nowhere was that task more vital and more central than in Muscovy. Muscovite boundaries at Peter's accession in 1682 must be viewed against the background of the Time of Troubles (1585–1613), when Muscovy was overrun and nearly extinguished by the Swedes and the Poles. It is so easy to forget that Peter's reign came but seventy years after this near disaster, years which badly scarred the Muscovite psyche. Those seventy years of Russian revival had been cruel ones; almost constant war was waged and the frontiers of Muscovy were in ferment and outward motion in the attempt of the new Romanov dynasty to justify itself on the throne of the Tsars by accomplishing the reconquest of Muscovite lands. Peter inherited the tradition of this reconquest, for on his accession the boundaries of his state were still not well established or permanently recognized by his bellicose neighbors.

By 1682 the Muscovite Tsardom had expanded from its patrimonial center in the forests of the upper Volga, and its growing armies had returned the Tsar's authority westward to a 600-mile armed frontier with Sweden and Poland-Lithuania which ran through Smolensk to Kiev. In all other directions the frontiers were fluid. To the north Muscovite authority went unchallenged among the few Finnish inhabitants of the bleak tundra and showed itself strongly only in the port of Archangel on the White Sea. To the east over the low hills of the Urals the Tsar's authority disappeared into the vast expanses of Siberia, where his will was proclaimed but hardly enforced. In the south Muscovy was still hundreds of miles from the Black Sea; in those territories of rich black soil the free Cossack frontiersmen in their autonomous communities on the Dnieper and the Don contested the waving grasslands with the Crimean Tatars, tributaries of the Ottoman Turk and the last remnant of the Mongol conquest. The only Muscovites here were peasants who had fled the growing pressures of Romanov absolutism to find some refuge.

Although Muscovy had survived and had reconquered many of the territories lost in the early years of the century, the reconquest was not complete nor the battle for survival completely over. Nowhere did the Muscovites abut water except tentatively on the far Pacific and on the northern Caspian; access to the open seas, to the Baltic and the Black, was still denied them, and the continental route to the rest of Europe was closed to them. The Muscovite Tsardom was moving to eradicate the sense of insecurity of the Troubled Times, to make permanent foreign recognition of its existence and its extent, to recover the Russian peoples still outside its expanding frontiers.

Consequently there was necessary movement in the military organization of Muscovy. The old military system was adapting itself to its role in the recovery of lands from the desperate, nearly fatal contest with Sweden and Poland. The motley crowds common in the early armies of national resurgence had given way after 1613 to the sixteenth-century system of semi-feudal armies, and these armies in turn proved ill-suited to the long and sustained campaigns which the expansion of Muscovy towards its old and distant borders now required. The levy of mounted landlords with a few armed attendants was an anachronism and was recognized as such in Moscow; the landlords hated to serve, demanded commands by precedence which they were incompetent to hold, came ill-equipped and ill-supplied, and chafed at campaigns which took them too far and too long from their estates. The permanent heart of the Muscovite army was the *streltsi*, or archers, the Tsar's bodyguards numbering some 20,000 men, and they were useless. Formed in the days of Ivan IV to protect the Tsar, they had been settled in Moscow as privileged, non-taxed, self-propagating townsmen with strong interests in crafts and commerce. The *streltsi* hated to leave the city, defended their privileges with far greater zeal than they defended their Tsar, and were riddled with the religious and social discontents then so common in Muscovite life.

The signs of movement in army organization came primarily in the "troops of foreign command," peasant conscripts officered by foreigners hired into service. These units bore heavily on an already strained treasury and were often too expensive to maintain in times of peace, but the authorities in Moscow had recognized long before Tsar Peter that permanent units recruited from the general population and properly trained and led were far superior to the hastily assembled and amateur nobility. Such units required conscription of peasants, and the practice was well under way by 1682; almost half of the army of 200,000 available to the Tsar in 1682 was in this form. The seventeenth-century "Tale of Savva Grudtsyn" noted that for the Smolensk campaign of 1634 "soldiers were to be recruited throughout all Russia . . . and when these recently recruited soldiers were transferred from Shuya to Moscow a German colonel continued their training." [1] Actually, only the nobles of Moscow Province managed to retain their sixteenth-century military formation into Peter's reign, while nobles from every other province were assigned to one of sixty regiments whose commanders were centrally appointed. These military developments could only benefit the monarchy.

The significant expansion of territories and of the military establishment in the seventeenth century was an outward sign and a substantial cause of the reemergence of Muscovite absolutism. The autocracy, generally described in European history textbooks as a permanent aspect of Muscovite society, was actually rebuilding since the emergence of an elected Romanov dynasty in 1613. The Time of Troubles, when the rule of Muscovite boyars dragged the state into defeat and chaos, had been proof enough for many of the need for a strong autocracy to balance the violently contesting forces of Muscovy. The Romanovs had capitalized on these bitter lessons to sup-

[1] "Tale of Savva Grudtsyn," in Serge A. Zenkovsky, ed., *Medieval Russia's Epics, Chronicles and Tales* (New York: E. P. Dutton & Co., Inc., 1963), pp. 386–88.

press institutions which might resist the monarch's will. As in other parts of Europe, absolutism was now justifying itself not by divine right but by its guarantee of earthly order and security. As a matter of fact, all across Europe monarchs were benefiting from reactions to troubled times which tended to prove the Hobbesian necessity of autocratic rule. Olearius of Holstein, observing this Muscovite development in the middle of the century, held that "the political government of Muscovy is monarchical and despotical. The Grand Duke is the hereditary monarch of it, and so absolute that no prince or lord in all his domains but thinks that it is an honor to assume the quality of his majesty's *kholop,* or slave."

The Tsardom was the unchallenged center of all executive, legislative and judicial authority, although those functions were still crudely organized and performed. The only remotely representative institution, the *zemskii sobor,* or Land Assembly, which had emerged from the chaos of the Troubles to elect the Romanov dynasty, suffered a fate strongly reminiscent of that of the Estates-General of France in the Hundred Years' War or that of the Church Councils after the election of Pope Martin V in 1415. No new dynasty enjoyed being reminded of its elective origins or enjoyed sharing power with such a body, and the meetings of the *zemskii sobor* grew less frequent as the Romanovs successfully pursued their work of reconquest, until it ceased to meet at all after 1654. The territorial successes of the new dynasty served to strengthen the absolutism of the state in innumerable ways. Since the central task of the new dynasty was the expulsion of the foreigner from its soil, military men were entrusted with the reconquest and were then properly rewarded with grants of estates and peasants in those territories in order to pacify and govern them. Thus the old forms of local government and provincial rights were swept away and state servants were imposed upon the land. War has always been the most satisfactory culture in which to breed an autocracy.

The military tasks of the seventeenth century naturally meant that the Muscovite government was in financial motion also, and the movement was in the direction of disaster. Financial crisis was the common condition of all active seventeenth-century monarchies, for everywhere the military and administrative ambitions of states galloped ahead of the exploitation of new financial resources to support them. The military tasks of the Romanov dynasty make it easy to see why the idea of a Tsar living off his own lands never survived the

Time of Troubles. In Moscow, as in Paris, the costs of war quadrupled during the century. The largest part of state revenues came from indirect taxes in the form of customs duties and state monopolies on certain products, and these were regularly increased. Direct taxation was becoming more simplified and more important as the costs of war were spread out over the general population; the old system of permitting government departments to levy and collect their own taxes for their own use passed away in 1679 before a unified household tax. Even with such simplification the journey of tax money from peasants to landlords to local agents to Moscow was a perilous one, for thievery took its toll at each passing of hands. It was a measure of the failure of a program which simply intensified older practices to meet new costs that the Tsars resorted more and more to emergency measures such as forced loans on such immensely wealthy enterprises as the Stroganovs, the family firm with interests in furs, salt, and many other products, and the Trinity Monastery, the most prestigious of the monastic establishments. The government also dimly recognized the need to increase the currency in circulation, a vital concern of Peter in later years, as Tsar Alexei began to issue copper rubles in 1656 until popular riots forced the withdrawal of this depreciated currency.

The reestablishment of central offices had taken place in this century largely to handle these increasing burdens of taxation, military organization, and pacification. But even in its central offices the autocracy had not articulated itself very well, and remained, in the words of Professor S. F. Platonov, a "system of delegation" wherein powers were passed by the Tsar to a trusted comrade, with the degree of power always dependent upon the personal trust of the ruler.[2] The primary office of Muscovite government was the *Boyar Duma*, the advisory council which had been expanding its membership consistently since 1613. Although still populated by members of old families of Moscow who claimed their posts by precedence, its expansion from 30 members in 1613 to almost 170 in 1682 had brought about the inclusion of more and more "new" notables invited by the Tsar to sit among his advisors. This drift surely reflected the new interests of the Muscovite Tsars in territories far distant from their city and indicated their desire to receive the counsels of those who shared their interests rather than those who claimed their seats by

[2] S. F. Platonov, "The Heritage of Muscovy," in Marc Raeff, ed., *Peter the Great: Reformer or Revolutionary?* (Boston, 1963), p. 4.

right. No enterprising European monarch has ever been satisfied to have his advisors chosen by any criterion except his own will.

The *Boyar Duma* became more unwieldy as its business grew, and it began the inevitable subdivision into special committees. The *Duma* itself met every morning to discuss policy on all matters of state business. Although there was some historical controversy about it, it now seems that the Tsar's *Duma* was no limitation on his authority but simply an extension of his autocratic power. Long before 1682 the power of the *Boyar Duma* was being shared with a group of the Tsar's favorites and confidants, and more and more the business of the *Duma* was performed not by graybeards who sat in silence to be deemed wise, but by their appointed and usually capable secretaries, the *diaki*.

The will of the Tsar and his *Duma* was carried out in practice through the *prikazi*, or departments. The word *prikaz*, "command," testifies to the origin and explains much of the difficulty of these departments. The Tsar's commands to boyars to carry out some specific task led to the establishment of an office. Such offices had grown haphazardly to more than 50 in number by the end of the century and overlapped badly in function; many of the *prikazi* had geographical rather than topical responsibilities and were thus in competition with other offices. Each *prikaz* had its own agents in the provinces, which created much proliferation and little administrative unity. By the end of the century these offices were in such disorder that Tsar Alexei established a special office to coordinate them "to the end that the Tsar's thoughts and acts be all fulfilled according to his wish." The attempt did not succeed. The *prikazi* were proof of the rule that efficiency of administration varied inversely with the distance from the person of the Tsar, and proof also of the crudity of an administration where that maxim would begin to be operative so very close to the throne. The haphazard growth of central administration in the wake of the reconquest was ripe for reorganization.

Local government was naturally the weakest link in the Muscovite system, as it was in almost every state across Europe, if only because it stood farthest from the Tsar. The Time of Troubles had served the autocracy well in this as in many other areas by destroying most remnants of local autonomy. The rebellions and the wars had crippled the ancient institutions of local government and enabled the Romanov dynasty to replace them with central appointments. The expansion of Muscovite authority demanded controls for the new acquisitions and the government answered with the expedient of military governors, *voievoda*. The appointment of such a military governor had formerly been called a "feeding," which indeed it was. The governor considered his appointment as a reward for service and a licence to line his pockets. His authority reflected that of the Tsar, "to act as is fitting in view of the business there, as God teaches." Military governors wielded far more extensive powers than were ever exercised by such officials as the *intendants* of France, since the autocracy faced no challenge in imposing them. By 1682 Muscovy had emerged in nine large military districts which provided Peter with the backbone of his first provincial reform.

One of the primary instruments for the organization of centralized monarchy has been the standardization of law. The feudal monarchs of western Europe, and one thinks here of Henry II of England and Philip II of France, had utilized unified law codes to usurp the judicial claims of their aristocratic rivals and thus to crush one of the formidable obstacles to their centralizing work. The Tsars of Muscovy underwent a similar experience except that this work, redone in the seventeenth century, was a bit easier than it had been in its original form under Ivan III and Ivan IV, since now older forms had already been swept away. The Code of 1649 issued by Tsar Michael was imposed on the areas of reconquest and signified the extension of Muscovite autocratic principle over forms of law alien to such principles; by 1682, for example, the oligarchic town forms of the Magdeburg law, popular in Lithuania and Poland, had been suppressed in favor of Muscovite absolutism.

The class structure of Muscovy was defined by the Code of 1649, which was designed by the new dynasty to restore order and hierarchy to a badly disordered society. But all law codes, being static descriptions of abstractions, are misleading guides to the tremors in any society. Townsmen were the smallest and weakest of the classes designated in the Code of 1649; only in the recovery of the seventeenth century did handicraft industries begin to center in towns which previously had been chiefly military or administrative centers, and such industries were besieged by competition from peasant "cottage" production in the countryside and privileged groups organized as military communities such as the *streltsi*. Townsmen were legally free but were a closed caste after 1649, with their status passing from father to son and their activities carefully circumscribed. These townsmen were beginning to push against the descriptions of the

Code and to make themselves felt in the growing market of this agricultural society. Their voices were heard rising in complaint through the *zemskii sobor* as early as 1642: "Sovereign, the trades among us your slaves have become worse in condition over the past few years because all our commerce in Moscow and the other towns has been taken over by many foreigners, Germans . . . , who arrive in Moscow and other towns with all manner of goods and sell them." Industry's sprouts were in mining, lumbering, salt production, and leather goods, but the sprouts were indeed low to the ground. Some nobles were organizing enterprises on their estates to increase their incomes, and there were even cases of peasant undertakings permitted by landlords which did well. The largest expansion of production came in handicraft industries in the small towns and peasant villages, meaning that the Muscovite population locally still tended its own needs.

The Muscovite government maintained a monopoly of foreign trade and never dreamed of surrendering it while its financial condition was so desperate. Naval stores, hides, and furs brought a substantial income from the Dutch and English merchants who controlled the carrying trade, and in this situation there had not been much movement since the sixteenth century. The Muscovites imported fine and rough cloths, furniture, weapons, and other consumer products. Both domestic and foreign trade were limited fields for native activity, due largely to the absence of a Muscovite merchant marine, interest in the sea, banking facilities, and credit systems; the money lenders in Muscovy were still the Church institutions, primarily the monasteries, which in the seventeenth century much preferred loans to land purchases and which charged exorbitant interest. The Dutch and the English, who benefited so substantially from such Muscovite disadvantages, never felt constrained to teach their customers any lessons in business practices. It was true also that the state was quite satisfied with the customs it harvested from the foreign merchants and would not endanger that income by any gambles on a hothouse Muscovite carrying company.

The Muscovite nobility on the eve of Peter's reign was disorganized and unworthy of the name: it had neither spiritual cohesion, corporate institutions, nor functional identification. Nobility was theoretically based on claims to a variety of ancestries such as descent from the Viking House of Rurik, which had provided the princes of the cities of old Kiev, or from the boyar aides of these princes, most of whom had been displaced by the expanding Muscovite Tsardom. There were as a result many more ancient families in the realm than the Romanovs, of whom the Golitsin and the Dolguruki clans were but two of the most ambitious. Then there were descendants of the many families who had allied with Muscovy or had been conquered and displaced from their original lands by Muscovite appointees, such as the princes of eastern Lithuania and the Tatar princes of Kazan and Astrakhan. But claim to ancestry was not as significant an identification of nobility as ownership of lands and serfs. Such owners obviously were sharply divided by wealth and by political influence; those closest to the Tsar tended to reap the rewards of estates and peasants, while those hidden in distant provinces struggled to survive on their tiny estates in conditions not sufficiently removed from those of their peasants to enable a visitor to tell the difference. The nobility only surfaced as a self-conscious company among those in permanent civil and military service and these were few in number, usually holders of estates in the neighborhood of Moscow, wealthy in lands, powerful in influence, and unwilling to admit that backwoods "nobles" had anything whatever in common with them.

Movement in the nobility of special significance for the Petrine reform was underway in the area of land tenure. Legally there were two types of land tenure for the nobility in seventeenth century Muscovy: *pomestie* and *votchina*. A *pomestie* estate was one held by a noble in return for service to the Tsar and was the device of Muscovite expansion in the fifteenth and sixteenth centuries and of the reconquest of the seventeenth; conquered lands were handed out to warriors to support their continued service. *Votchina* was land held by a noble by right of inheritance for which he owed no service and which could be passed on to his heirs; such tenure was of ancient vintage. These two legally different tenures seemed to indicate two types of nobles: those who depended on service to the state for their status and those who were independent of the state in their wealth. But the law disguised a very different and complex reality. Many historians have said that *pomestie* was relapsing into *votchina* during the seventeenth century, but that does not tell the whole story. Actually, *pomestie* and *votchina* were beginning to coalesce, a movement of significance in directing the Petrine reform, and therefore to be examined.

Pomestie estates were originally grants to nobles for their lifetimes or for as long as they were in service, and were then returnable to the state for redistribution to other useful crown servants. But human nature was hard at work, and the urge of the *pomeshchiks* to secure the inheritance of their lands for their sons rather than to surrender them to the state at their death or retirement was extremely strong. The Muscovite government of the seventeenth century was deeply in debt to these *pomeshchiks,* for they were the leaders of the armies of reconquest and the administrators of the territories when they were indeed reconquered. Therefore the state permitted them to make their heirs co-holders during their lifetimes and thus assure their continuation on the property. In the same spirit some *pomeshchiks* were even exchanging, selling, or mortgaging their estates as if the lands were their own in perpetuity. By the second half of the century, *pomeshchiks* had acquired substantial control of their property to use and dispose of it, which was not yet legally recognized but never officially forbidden. The government in Moscow insisted only that whoever was benefiting from the estate's income should continue to render civil or military service to the state.

At the same time *votchina* tenure was in the process of change in the opposite direction. Hereditary nobles, masters of their own lands and peoples, would have been, in the French or English experience, at the root of resistance to the centralizing absolutism of the seventeenth century. But, by the second half of the century, the nobility of Muscovy with inherited rights to land had really forfeited any chance to challenge the crown. There was no practice of primogeniture, an absence notable in the Rhineland in the Middle Ages with many of the same consequences: inherited estates were constantly sub-divided among heirs, plots became smaller and smaller and consequently unable to bear a noble above subsistence level. Heirs of such families receiving their meager allotments of property could only turn to the Tsar in this century of conquest and apply for grants of lands and serfs to maintain themselves; such grants, of course, carried service requirements. Pleas to the Tsar Michael revealed the plight of these nobles: "Sire, be merciful to us, your poor slaves, ruined and helpless, without *pomestie* . . . , and endow us with a *pomestie* or a grant of money." *Votchina,* or inherited tenure, existed only in the law and usually only as a partial holding of any particular noble. Most hereditary nobles held some land for service even if they avoiding performing it, and the real difference between the legal forms must be considered minimal.

It was also true that the increasing imposition of state service on the nobility during the seventeenth century served to distract some of them from their ancestral lands and to encourage their transfer, or at least their involvement, in other parts of the realm. This was a consummation which any monarch of the age would devoutly wish as it set the precedent for separating nobles from their seats of power, a task which Louis XIV had to work at much harder than did Tsar Peter. At the same time, the Muscovite nobility weakened itself in internal competition based on rules of precedence, which held that a man ought never to accept a government post less exalted than that held by any of his ancestors. This practice was manifestly a barrier to the rise and reward of talent in the nobility, which had to be dealt with if the state was ever to meet its major new manpower problems. The seventeenth century helped clear the way for Peter in this regard; one device of his Romanov forebears was to appoint "precedence posts" in Moscow as honorary commands and to give the field commands on the basis of talent. Since the intricate system of precedence was based on registers which began to be kept in 1475, it was relatively simple to end it once the determination was made; Tsar Fyodor ordered the registers burned in 1682 and cleared another legal obstacle to the Petrine reform. Fyodor could not, of course, burn out the conviction of some noble families that government service was their exclusive preserve by right of heritage.

By 1682, then, the Muscovite nobility was in important but as yet unguided movement toward becoming an identifiable group with certain characteristics in common: serf and land ownership, unofficial but operative inheritance rights, theoretical if inoperative obligations to service, and access to state positions legally based on talent rather than blood. The major steps in the Petrine reform of the nobility had already been taken. More important now than any distinctions of tenure rights were distinctions between nobles of wealth and influence and nobles who shirked service and struggled for survival on their tiny plots. The first group ran the Muscovite government, but most obstacles to moving the second group forcibly into it had been removed.

Under the control of this emerging nobility worked the bulk of the Muscovite population—the peasantry. The Soviet economic historian Lyashchenko wrote that "the agrarian order and rural economy serve as the key to the understanding of all economic and social relationships within the feudal economy and society of Moscow state during the sixteenth and seventeenth centuries." If we avoid that historical hornet's nest as to what is "feudal" and what is not, we can at least agree without much difficulty that Muscovy was an agricultural economy and that the central fact of serfdom in that economy has a great deal to do with explaining the society. The "peasantry" of the sixteenth and early seventeenth centuries had actually never been as monolithic as the term peasantry always seems to imply, and represented many groups with differing rights and differing conditions of life and service: private serfs in farming or in domestic service, military colonists on the frontiers, state peasants working on government lands, church peasants usually on monastery lands, free peasants who often enough employed others, rent-paying tenants and share-croppers, agricultural laborers who worked for others, peasants with letters of permission to practice crafts in towns, wandering beggars and migrant workers, and even slaves. Yet, in the seventeenth century there was movement here, too, and it was all in the direction of abolishing these distinctions among the peasants and driving them all toward state and private serfdom.

Serfdom prevailed in the southern and western parts of European Russia, a fact explained by the two forces which lay behind serfdom in the first place. These were fertile lands where a decent living in agriculture could be made and where landlords were interested in maintaining and controlling a labor force. These were also the lands into which Muscovy had expanded by handing estates over to *pomeshchiks* in reward for services and in expectation of local administration. To be valuable, these estates had to be populated with workers, and serfdom was the state's instrument for maintaining its civil and military servants. The Code of 1649 bound the serf to the land, not to the landlord. State peasants, working on lands controlled by some government office, were, in a sense, enserfed to the state. They predominated in the northern and central provinces; their condition was substantially better than that of private serfs, since they enjoyed an abstract and absentee landlord and were customarily supervised by peasant stewards much like themselves.

Throughout the seventeenth century serf status in one of the above forms was steadily expanding over many other peasant groups in the society, if only because it was in the reorganizing state's interest to pin down its taxpayers and conscripts to specific places under close controls. The laws dragged far behind this reality. The *pomeshchik* class had grown substantially, with estates carved out of the re-conquest and the movement into the Ukraine after 1654. The state conferred steadily growing powers on the landlords, manifesting its reliance on them for pacifying the peasantry and for collecting taxes from them. Older economic forces were also at work, those forces generated by any troublous time when peasants must go into debt to repair the ravages of war and to deliver excessive rents to military conquerors. Peasants in the wake of rebellions and wars had to borrow, and debts served to erode those rights of movement and free labor that distinguished many peasant groups from serfs. The state had no real interest in resisting such a drift or in continuing to distinguish groups in the peasantry save private and state serfs, not out of any malice but simply because the state's primary concern with them as conscripts and taxable souls was more efficiently served in simple categories and less expensive in *pomeshchik* hands.

The conditions of agricultural life in Muscovy, as in every part of Europe, seemed eternally unchanging. Peasants still labored with wooden or iron plows and scythes to raise a small variety of grains, while horses and oxen still provided manure as well as power. Any increase in Muscovite agricultural production in the seventeenth century was the result of the expansion of the amount of land in cultivation rather than of new techniques. As a matter of fact, older and more restrictive forms which would have disintegrated of their own uselessness in this century were actually preserved by outside intervention. The communal repartitioning of land, designed to periodically reshuffle land equitably among families, was breaking down as more successful peasants developed their properties; but the poorer peasants and the state itself intervened to force the redistribution of lands in order to keep all peasants in at least minimum taxpaying status. Such intervention helped to destroy what little peasant initiative there was, as energetic farmers saw their hard work handed over to those hardly equipped to carry it on.

As the pressures within this agricultural system mounted, the only alternatives for peasants were patient suffering, flight, or rebellion, and all three were present in abundance in seventeenth-century Muscovy. The lands in the east, north, and south all attracted runaways, for neither state nor serfdom had yet made their presence felt in the steppes, in the tundra, or in Siberia. The population of Siberia at the end of the seventeenth century was probably about 300,000, of which perhaps one quarter were Russian, although their numbers were increasing. Revolts were not as common as runaways but they were common enough. The peasant wars of the Time of Troubles were followed by the salt riots of the 1640's, the rising of Vasili Us in 1666, and the sweeping southern revolt of Stenka Razin in 1670. A contemporary recalled of the forces of Razin that "the rebellious Cossacks travel through the provinces and massacre the *pomeshchiks* and the *votchiniks* who own peasants, but they do not rob or kill the black peasants[3] . . . nor any other serving people." Naturally, the Muscovite government was preoccupied with peasant revolts which had characterized the Time of Troubles and which threatened its future, which explains the total reliance on the *pomeshchiki*. Such preoccupation was reflected in the Code of 1649 which devoted a large section to rebellions: "Should any person in the Muscovite state . . . learn of the existence of any unrest or any plot or any evil plan, he must report them either to the Tsar Alexei Mikhailovich or to . . . local governors. . . ."

Describing Muscovite society in the seventeenth century, travelers' accounts in western Europe emphasized the exotic and barbaric qualities of life, the long beards and flowing robes that seemed to smack of distant Asia, the rampant cruelties, the heavy drinking, the grotto-like churches so distant from western European tastes, the complex and perplexing Orthodox ritual, the idolatrous reverence for icons, and the overwhelming absolutism. Beginning with such surface evaluations, foreign observers and historians for centuries to come would label Muscovite culture as stagnant, static, unproductive, hieratic, a one-way avenue into a cul-de-sac. "Stagnant" and "static" were particularly inappropriate words, for the culture of Muscovy was in substantial motion beneath its ritual surface. It was true that Muscovite culture tended to be self-contained and heavily religious in nature; Wladimir Weidlé called it a "horizontal culture" in which the people played a large role and in which the hierarchy of intellectuals and people was not well marked. The apparent xenophobia among Muscovites, for example, their resentment of foreigners and foreign ways, which was common to most of the lower classes across Europe, was in Muscovy not a lower- versus upper-class phenomenon but a feeling shared by peasant, merchant, priest, and noble.

In the early seventeenth century the Orthodox Church was at the center of Russian culture. That fact alone certainly did not set Muscovy apart from most European national histories. The Church, however, far more than in most states of Europe except perhaps England,

---

[3] "Black peasants" were not subject to private landlords.

had become closely associated with national independence. The Russian Orthodox Church was the only branch of the Eastern Church still associated with an Orthodox government; all the other autocephalous pieces had fallen under the sway of Moslem Turks or Catholic Germans. There were traditions of the "Third Rome" from the fifteenth century, then as now badly misunderstood in western Europe, and of an independent Patriarchate since 1589, but these memories were scarcely as important as the role of the Orthodox Church in leading the national resurgence since the Time of Troubles. As a result of that role the Church had enjoyed a vigorous religious revival in the early seventeenth century, especially observable in monastic life, and church and state had cooperated rather harmoniously in pressing the expulsion of the Poles and Swedes; it was no obstacle to their cooperation that Muscovy's enemies were at the same time both politically dangerous and religiously repugnant. The political and religious role of Patriarch Philaret, father of Tsar Michel, was living proof of the Church's ascendancy.

But it is still a serious mistake to consider that Muscovite religious life was static and stable and that it therefore underlay a static and stable culture. The Church and its place in society were under severe challenge in the seventeenth century, a challenge which intensified as the century progressed, from forces of religious reform on one side and forces of secular reform on the other. Those acquainted with the European Reformation will not find that combination of attackers peculiar. The most critical event in the history of the Russian Orthodox Church, and possibly the most critical event in Muscovite history, was the annexation of Ukraine. It is not terribly important to analyze the exact intent of the Periaslavl Agreement of 1654 between Tsar Alexei and the Hetman Hmelnetsky of the Little Russians, nor even to understand the precise terms of Muscovy's Treaty of Andrusovo with Poland in 1667, to know that between 1640 and 1667 Muscovite authority moved into the black soil of Ukraine east of the River Dnieper and reclaimed the "lost lands" and the capital of Kiev.

The annexation of Ukraine was significant in one sense because it brought within the boundaries of Muscovy a full-scale intellectual and religious ferment. Ukraine had been, since the opening of the Catholic Counter-Reformation of the sixteenth century, one of the prime targets of Jesuit attention through the intermediary of the Poles. The "Uniate Church," a combination of eastern ritual and Roman allegiance, was used in these lands to win new converts from

Orthodoxy. Jesuit infiltration, seen at its most dramatic in the Mussorgsky opera *Boris Godunov*, had been resisted during the Polish occupation of western Ukraine by two quite opposite but equally effective means—Cossack wars and a vigorous intellectual revival. A struggle within the Ukrainian clergy as to whether or not to adopt Jesuit methods against the Uniate Church was lost by the "old guard," and the Kievan Academy was founded in 1631 by Peter Moghila. This dynamic cleric, former abbot of the Monastery of the Crypt and later Metropolitan of Kiev, made his Academy the educational center of Orthodoxy, responsible for what Professor James Billington calls "the theological arming of the Russian clergy." [4] The Academy adopted Polish form and Jesuit techniques to teach its clergy theology, apologetics, sermon writing, and public speaking. The academy turned out a generation of scholar-clergymen who spread across eastern Europe radiating their talents, training, and enthusiasm into the Orthodox world. It was this group which came in a steady stream into Muscovy in the seventeenth century, and from which the Petrine church was ultimately staffed. These men, educated and progressive, hated irrationalism, superstition, ignorance, and disorder and saw these forces as fatal to the future of Orthodoxy.

This Ukrainian influx of Latin learning did not go unchallenged. In 1652 a dynamic young Muscovite clergyman from the Trans-Volga region, the ancient fortress of Muscovite spirituality since the days of Nilus of Sorsk, became Patriarch of the Russian Church. Patriarch Nikon, six feet six inches tall and only forty-seven at his appointment, had already been Abbot of the Novospassky Monastery and Metropolitan of Novgorod. In the early years his influence with Tsar Alexei was enormous, even to the point of conferring with him on important government matters. Nikon's feelings toward Ukrainian developments were ambivalent; as a member in his youth of the Muscovite party of Church reform he could only sympathize with its educational aims, but he could not sympathize with its Latin Catholic models. For Nikon the true sources of Orthodox reform were to be found in the ancient Greek traditions of the Church fathers. For Nikon the only successful route to the restoration of the purity of faith and the protection from the secular attacks of the age was not compromise with the enemies but reattachment to the Greek roots of Orthodoxy.

At the same time, Nikon emerged as a proponent of Church auton-

[4] James H. Billington, *The Icon and the Axe* (New York: Alfred A. Knopf, Inc., 1967), p. 127.

omy, holding that the church must be recognized at least as the partner of the state if it were to survive and prosper. Here too, Nikon looked to the Greek heritage, where Emperor and Patriarch harmoniously governed the body and soul of mankind. So, in ritual and politics the new Patriarch brought the forces of Greek scholarship, even those carefully circumscribed and guarded scholars whom he selected from Ukraine, to bear upon the problems of Russian Orthodoxy. His first target was the meaningless jargon which passed for Church ritual after centuries of neglect and decay, and he intended to purify and restore the true meaning and form of the Slavonic ritual. The words and gestures had lost their significance through centuries of use by an ignorant clergy and an illiterate people, and practices foreign to the pattern of Eastern Orthodoxy had grown up unchecked in Muscovy. Worse, these foreign practices had been incorporated and hallowed in the Muscovite popular faith during its prolonged isolation from the Orthodox world, until the mistakes, corruptions, and additions were considered part of the untouchable quality of the true faith. In the light of such developments, Nikon's program might seem sensible enough: who would not support the correction and reform of a great faith according to its origins in order to strengthen it against the foreign compromises of Ukraine and the political encroachments of the state? But the work was confounded by two serious difficulties: the Muscovite psychology and the Nikonian personality.

The Muscovite people valued form above content; that is to say, they venerated the way in which the ritual was performed far more than the meaning of the words and practices themselves. It has been said of Muscovy that this reverence for external appearances was deeply imbedded in all aspects of life, and we shall have reason to see something of it at work in the popular resistance to Peter the Great's social reforms. Too much can be made of the peculiarity of this trait to Muscovy, however, for no one has ever been bold enough to describe any branch of the European peasantry in the seventeenth century or any other century as oriented to theology rather than ritual or to meaning rather than form. As a matter of fact, anyone who paid attention to the effects of the ritual reforms in the Roman Catholic Church brought about by the Vatican Council II in the second half of the twentieth century will generate far more sympathy for the Muscovites of the seventeenth. In any case, Nikon's attempts to reform the rituals encountered violent opposition. Attacks upon the ways of a faith good enough for fathers and their fathers before them and defended and enshrined through years of bitter foreign wars could only be viewed as a vicious attack of Protestants or Catholics upon the fabric of the true faith, an insidious conspiracy to drive Christ from His only earthly home. Nikon's attempts to defend the ancient faith against the secularist state and the rationalist Kievans were badly misunderstood and unappreciated by the Muscovite population, and introduced a terribly divisive cleavage between intellectual elite and the popular faith. Those who have been impressed thus far with parallels with the German Reformation had best note that here the reform had no popular base.

Some historians have been unable to restrain themselves from seeing in Nikon the forerunner of Peter, depicting both as reformers inspired by "western thought" to impose a pure and rational order on ancient and irrational practices, by force if necessary; indeed rumors were rife in Peter's lifetime that he was the illegitimate son of the reforming Patriarch. Such a view is badly misleading: Nikon was not trying to secularize society, but trying to save society from secularization by girding the Orthodox faith for the modern battles with the state and with Latin learning. He was not so much a product of Kievan education as a reaction against its implications. And surely there was an immense distance between the "western thought" in which Nikon found his inspiration and that favored by the Tsar Peter. If anyone was a "defensive reformer," trying to reshape the Orthodox faith in order to save it from the attacks of the new age, it was Nikon. But it was true that Nikon made Peter's work easier, for he unintentionally ruptured the fabric of Church authority, undermined popular attachment to the Church, and left the official Church a hollow shell with little power of resistance for the battles yet to come. The major step toward the secularization of Muscovite culture was the weakening of the hold of Church authority over that culture, and for that weakening Nikon was really more responsible than Peter.

At the same time the personality of Patriarch Nikon was his undoing. He was a tough-minded, imperious individual who in theory preached the equality and harmony of church and state powers but who in practice acted like an autocrat himself. At one point even the gentle Tsar Alexei called Nikon "Great Sovereign," a title last borne by a churchman in the days of Philaret. Nikon issued his reforming decrees at a council in 1654, the Patriarch of Constantinople affirmed them, and a committee of scholars began the revisions of the ritual. But even as his work went on the Patriarch Nikon lost his post. In 1658 the Tsar Alexei finally moved against the priest's political presumptions. It was ironic that the Church councils of 1666 and 1667, attended by the Tsar and several of the eastern patriarchs, at the same time approved the deposition of Nikon and the implementation of his reforms.

Muscovy reacted violently against the Nikonian reforms. Leadership of popular resistance came from poorer clergy and from members of the hiararchy such as the heroic Archpriest Avakkum. Avakkum was far closer in spirit to Nikon than might be expected, for they shared an early association and a common goal to keep the Orthodox faith central in Muscovite society and free from foreign taint; but Avakkum could not believe that this goal would ever be attained by undermining the forms of popular faith and shaking the piety and allegiance of the people. Spiritual resistance necessarily became physical resistance once the state decreed enforcement of the reforms, and soon many of the lower clergy and the faithful were in flight from a Church they considered in heresy and a state which had made itself an accessory to the crime. These refugees came to be known as *raskolninki* (schismatics) or *staroveri* (Old Believers), and many of them fled to the frontiers to provide havens for the true faith. The Archpriest Avakkum, severely persecuted and finally burned in 1682, left a powerful legacy in his *Autobiography:* "Until the time of Nikon the Apostate, under our pious Princes and Tsars, we had pure Orthodoxy in Russia and a non-seditious church. Nikon the Wolf decreed with the Devil that we should make the sign of the cross with three fingers. . . ." Monasteries where the Old Belief was harbored were besieged and purged. Many of those who attached themselves publicly to the Old Belief did so for reasons as much political and economic as spiritual: the peasants resentful of their landlords, the merchants resentful of state tolerance of foreigners, intellectuals resentful of the secular influences being embraced by some Church leaders. And how many who did not defect publicly from the official Church did so in their secret hearts we do not know.

The reasons for the Tsar's enforcement of the Nikonian reforms and for insistence on his primacy over the Patriarch do indeed have Byzantine precedents, but they seem hardly as important as the general claim of European monarchs in this age of war to exclusive political allegiance and exclusive control of the resources of their kingdoms. Monarchs all over Europe, Catholic as well as Protestant, reaped a reward from the Reformation in increased control over the Church and its resources, and the same might be said of the experience of the Russian Tsar with his own Church reform. The claims of the Church to separate allegiance of the people could not be countenanced nor its lands and peoples and wealth permitted to remain outside the taxing and conscripting authority of the Tsar in the emergencies of the seventeenth century. Alexei did not himself directly move against Church wealth, except to temporarily redirect its income and to impose forced loans, but he forged the conditions by which such movement became possible.

If the Church's defenses were deteriorating from within, secular forces were also active in pushing it from its central role in Muscovite society. There is a substantial debate about the literacy rate in pre-Petrine Muscovy; the inbred reaction of most "western" historians has been to respond immediately that Muscovites were obviously vastly illiterate. But the presence of popular books and pamphlets in the seventeenth century would indicate a higher rate of literacy than has been allowed. The clergy coming out of Ukraine after 1640 were primarily responsible for any advance in secular education for the laity. A noble established a monastery for thirty Kievan monks at Moscow in 1649 in order to have them teach. In 1666 Simon Polotsky and his student Sylvester Medvedyev opened a Latin Academy, and in 1683 the Printing Office established a school which annually registered over two hundred students. Later on, Medvedyev's Academy and the Printing Office merged into the Slavonic-Greek-Latin Academy which provided a battlefield for Greek and Latin learning. The Latins won, since Constantinople simply could not compete with Kiev in providing able teachers. Similar educational developments were taking place at Troitsa Monastery, at Novgorod, and at Kharkov.

Language and literature were also in flux. The state required a simple secular language to do the business of modern government; this was the so-called "chancellery language," based on the spoken language of Muscovy. The standard reading fare of the century remained saints' lives and the oral tradition still flourished, but the secularization of literature was coming apace. In forms filtering through Ukraine, Poland, the Balkans, and even Persia came adventure stories, romantic epics, morality plays, and even satires. "Frol Skobeev the Rogue" satirized the man of the new age who skillfully manipulated his way through a world which no longer cherished the ancient virtues.

The forces of change were strong in architecture and the arts as well. The homes of boyars and bureaucrats were becoming fit subjects for architecture, a sure sign of the emergence of secular values, even though the asymmetrical piles of buildings represented in the Stroganov Palace at Solvychegodsk and the Tsar's summer palace at Kolomenskoe seem far closer to the medieval home of Jacques Coeur at Bourges than to the Renaissance palaces of the Medici or the Frescobaldi. Monumental architecture was symbolic, too, for it was the state which was now being glorified: the Golden Gate of Moscow was rebuilt, the Moscow Kremlin towers retopped, and the governmental centers in many cities refurbished. In the second half of the century the baroque style arrived from Ukraine, and rapidly developed into a distinctive form of government and religious architecture. Even the ancient art of icon painting was being secularized in both style and purpose: the Tsar's Icon Painters at the Oruzhenia Palace directed by Simon Ushakov showed new concern with anatomy and perspective, and their work was often intended for the domestic decoration of wealthy bureaucrats and merchants.

Perhaps the most concentrated form of secular influence was found in the German, or Foreign, Quarter of Moscow. The presence of so many foreigners in trade and military service had begun to frighten the common folk, annoy the Church authorities, and antagonize the Muscovite merchants. In order to preserve the Orthodox from contamination by foreign heresies and habits and to lessen the friction among his subjects aroused by their presence, Tsar Alexei decreed the establishment of a Foreign Quarter in the suburbs of Moscow where these foreigners would be compelled to make their homes. What such a decree created, of course, was a tiny microcosm which reflected the tastes and achievements of the few wealthy states on the Atlantic seaboard deep into the heart of continental Muscovy.

The whole drift of internal and external policy, the expansion of the absolutist state, the constant frontier wars, the internal struggles of church and peasantry, the emergence of a secular culture, all represented Muscovy's growing role in the amalgamation of Europe. If the characteristics of early modern Europe might be rapidly summarized as the emergence of the nation-state, the centralization of the monarchy, the creation of the bureaucracy, the all-European quality of warfare, the triumph of state over dynastic foreign policy, the shaping of a European market, the carving out of empires, and the flourishing of a secularized learning, then Muscovy must not be set apart from this European age. The words of Gustavus Adolphus about war, quoted by Professor James Billington, apply as well to most forces at work in Europe: "All European wars are being interwoven into one knot, are becoming one universal war." [5] It is far more sensible, I think, to consider that Muscovy was joining other European states in the emergence of the modern European world than to pose Muscovy as outside of and opposed to some monolithic unity called "Europe" or "the west." There are many Europes and many "western" traditions, and in the seventeenth century these many European styles and many "western" traditions were being communicated one to the other as never before. Muscovy was deeply involved in that communication, and would soon be more so. Does one call this "westernization"? Readily, if one agrees that Sweden, Austria, Poland, Italy, Spain, and the rest were being in some sense "westernized" at the same time. After such an admission it becomes much less a mystical undertaking to investigate the differences in national development among the European states. It was within this framework of amalgamation and communication of all-European forms that Tsar Peter came to reign and to which he committed Muscovy more deeply and consciously than many another "European" state.

[5] Billington, *op. cit.*, p. 117.

※ 2 ※

The Education to Power

The monarchs of Europe's early modern age shared a precarious youth; thus they reflected through their early years the political and social instabilities of the era against which their later absolutist policies were directed. Louis XIV had his *frondes*, the Great Elector his Thirty Years' War, Charles XI of Sweden his regency, and Charles II of England his exile. So also the years from Peter the Great's birth in 1672 to the outbreak of the Great Northern War in 1700 were incredibly active and perilous ones; in those years, as the Tsar grew to young manhood, he lived through three coups d'état, constant threats of violence against his family, seven years of semi-exile, his first military campaigns, an unprecedented journey to western Europe, and a major revolt against his rule. From these bitter personal experiences, these painful political struggles, and these tentative approaches to war and government, Peter slowly learned the strengths and weaknesses of his heritage.

Peter's birth was itself an important factor in the political struggles which dominated his early years and the whole of the eighteenth century. The Tsar Alexei was married twice. Maria Miloslavsky, his first wife, who died in 1669, had in customary fashion provided entry for her large family into the Muscovite government with all its perquisites. Two male heirs of this marriage, Fyodor and Ivan, survived to guarantee the continuation of the Miloslavsky clan in its benefices. But the widowed Tsar Alexei grew lonely in his middle age and an advisor, Artamon Matveev, arranged a second marriage for the Tsar with his ward, Natalia Naryshkin, in 1671. This marriage displaced the Miloslavsky from their posts of power at court and in-

troduced a host of Naryshkin relatives in their place, and it also
presented the state with a parallel line of succession in the boy Peter
who was born of this marriage.

The rivalry between the families of the first and second wives of
Tsar Alexei was natural and deep, and it was aggravated anew when
Tsar Alexei died in 1676 and his eldest son by the first marriage,
Fyodor, took the throne. The Naryshkins were displaced by Fyodor
and his Miloslavsky relatives; they were forced into retirement and
Artamon Matveev was banished to Archangel. Still, Tsar Fyodor was
a sickly type and his brother and logical heir, Ivan, added mental incompetence to the family problems. Their half-brother Peter, on the
other hand, was growing into a tall, strong, excessively healthy young
man whose very existence was a reproach and a threat to the
Miloslavsky maintenance of power.

Tsar Fyodor died on April 27, 1682, and the Naryshkin clan leaped
into the vacuum to nominate the boy Peter as the next Tsar, intending
thereby to set aside the Miloslavsky candidate, Ivan, and all the
Miloslavsky relatives with him. Patriarch Joakhim, a loyal Naryshkin
ally, gave his blessing and a crowd of Muscovites, grandiosely but un-
scrupulously labeled a *zemski sobor*, an assembly of the people,
hailed Peter as Tsar. But naming a Tsar was not maintaining him;
force would be required to insure the succession for Peter and the
invocation of force opened a Pandora's box that would take eight
years to close. The instrument of force and the key to the struggle of
the families was the Tsar's bodyguard, the *streltsi*.

The *streltsi* were a miserable and vacillating group and the title of
Tsar's bodyguard does them too much semantic honor. They had

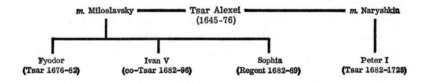

been little interested in guarding since the Time of Troubles; their
privileges in trade in the city of Moscow served them too well
financially. About 20,000 in number, their self-recruiting regiments
drew in peasants from the countryside, often runaway serfs, to swell
their ranks; thus they represented the rural attitudes of Muscovy

as well as the political passions of the Kremlin. The Naryshkin party purchased their help in the coup of 1682 with abundant promises of money, redress of grievances against their officers, curtailment of the rights of foreigners to trade in the city, and a more sympathetic view of the Old Belief. All this constituted quite a reactionary policy. It would be a great mistake, therefore, to think that the Naryshkins were seeking power as any progressive force for the renovation of Muscovy; just the opposite was the case. Peter had taken no part in elevating himself to the sovereign title, for he was but ten years old. This was the victory of a self-seeking family.

The Miloslavsky party slowly recovered its equilibrium, and its spokesman in the wake of the Naryshkin coup of 1682 was a woman, the Tsarevna Sophia, twenty-five-year-old daughter of Tsar Alexei. Sophia was fat and ugly, but ambitious, clever, and determined. It was her policy for the moment to press the claims of her weakling brother Ivan as the legitimate heir, since he was both the elder of the two boys and the representative of the senior branch of the Romanovs; Sophia would have power over Ivan V and, through him, over Muscovy. With the assistance of Ivan Miloslavsky, her uncle, and of Ivan Khovansky, a popular *streltsi* commander and leader of the Old Belief, she began a campaign among the *streltsi* to convince them that they had been badly deceived, that Matveev, far from willing to limit foreign merchants and restore the Old Belief, was himself an adherent of western heresies. Sophia supplied heavy doses of money, religious propaganda, and alcohol to the *streltsi* until they became a rampaging instrument of violence.

The stimulus to the *streltsi* revolt was a rumor, assiduously propagated by Sophia, that the Naryshkins had murdered little Ivan. In May the *streltsi* repeatedly invaded and drunkenly ravaged the Kremlin grounds. On May 17 Natalia finally tried to stop the rioting by appearing on the porch of the Faceted Palace to show both Ivan and Peter alive. But the rebels were too drunken and incensed to be placated and, in the sight of Peter and his mother, seized Matveev and two Naryshkin uncles and tossed them over the stairway to their deaths on waiting pikes below. The *streltsi* then turned to riot in the city. This aimless bloodbath seemed an urban echo of the immense peasant upheavals of the century. Some historians have insisted with much justice that Peter never forgot this terrorizing experience and was thenceforth intent on avoiding Moscow, and that the founding of Saint Petersburg thus had its roots in these riots. The events had much in common with the experiences of young Louis XIV with his *frondes*, which may likewise have been influential in driving the monarchy from riotous Paris.

Sophia was in shaky control. Her new arrangement was without precedent in Muscovite history: two Tsars were declared, Ivan V as senior Tsar and Peter I as junior Tsar, with Sophia as Regent. The Soviets still exhibit in the armory of the Kremlin a perfect symbol of these years, the double throne with the hidden seat behind it from which Sophia whispered instructions to her young figureheads. Sophia announced that God had inspired this arrangement, but others thought that Vasili Golitsin, the wealthy and sophisticated lover of the Regent, had more to do with it. Golitsin emerged as the prime force in her government, while Ivan Khovansky was made *streltsi* commander.

But Sophia's control was far from secure. The *streltsi* had tasted power and played a heady role as Tsar-makers; they were not ready to reassume their former place. They staged a rally in the Kremlin Square on the merits of the Old Belief, during which the Regent Sophia herself was threatened. The *streltsi* pressed more serious demands upon Sophia as the price of their continued support, including a purge of her advisors and the right to allot punishments in the city. Even Khovansky, entrusted with the good behavior of the *streltsi*, seemed now filled with secret ambitions to rule for himself in Moscow. Sophia and her lover fled the city and issued a call to all boyars and foreign troops to join them. The *streltsi* seized the Kremlin and only when Sophia's forces had surrounded the city in early October and manifested clear control did the rebels agree to terms. Some of the *streltsi* leaders were executed, others were exiled, while most took the oath to the Regent. Only when peace was solidly restored in early November did Sophia return to the capital. And through all the terror and anarchy of 1682, the little Tsar Peter cowered wide-eyed and petrified with fear. Such was his initiation into the world of Muscovite politics.

These events of 1682 signified no great confrontation of policy about the direction of Muscovy; rather they signified the personal quality of Muscovite government and the violent ambitions of her great families. At the same time it was clear to some observers that the *streltsi* organization was impossible and could not long be permitted to paralyze politics or bear primary responsibility for national defense. Further, the struggles of 1682, as Professor Michael Florinsky has pointed out, floated on the surface of the deep resentments of seventeenth-century

Muscovy: of Schismatics against the Church reforms, of townsmen against successful foreign merchants in their midst, and even of peasants against the growing burdens of serfdom. In all, the events of 1682 reflected the general reaction of many Muscovites to the pressures of the emerging Romanov state.

Between 1682 and 1689 Muscovite history actually proceeded in two parallel lines and then reconverged: one line was that of government policy and the other that of Peter's development outside the mainstream of state activity. These years of Sophia's Regency have been reevaluated by Professor C. B. O'Brien, and we are now able to see that the adherents of Sophia and Vasili Golitsin constituted the forward-looking party, interested in finding affirmative answers to the domestic and foreign problems left by the seventeenth century.[1] It was, oddly enough, Peter's party, led by his mother Natalia and the Patriarch Joakhim, which represented the forces of obscurantism and reaction. It is vital to an understanding of the growing drift of loyalty from Sophia to the Naryshkin camp in these years to appreciate the conservative attitudes which Natalia Naryshkin espoused against her activist opponent.

The policies of Sophia and Golitsin mingled strong strains of personal ambition with broad visions of the Muscovite future. Clearly, Sophia wished to make her authority in Muscovy permanent and to share supreme power with her lover. But the task of assuming the crown for herself and Golitsin was not easy; no woman had ever ruled in the Russian lands and the tradition of female seclusion was still strong. Vasili Golitsin was himself a controversial figure, and was known to favor foreign ways. The pair knew that their road to the throne must be carefully mapped. Golitsin charted this route through the external glory of Muscovy in league with foreign powers against the infidel Turk, and foresaw in the wake of such a victory the internal enlightenment of Muscovy. This would seem sufficient to replace two children on the throne, one of whom was a mental defective and the other an apolitical giant.

The abilities of Vasili Golitsin were central to the ambitions of this pair; whoever said that politics made strange bedfellows must surely have had these two in mind. Golitsin was educated and urbane, speaking Latin, German, and French with ease. His program, which the

[1] C. B. O'Brien, *Russia Under Two Tsars 1682–1689, The Regency of Sophia Alekseevna* (Berkeley: University of California, 1952).

historian Paul Miliukov labeled magnificent vision but disastrous politics, deserves attention in itself and as a touchstone for the later work of Peter. Golitsin believed that Muscovy needed a regular army to displace the influence of the nobility and the *streltsi;* he foresaw permanent diplomatic and commercial ties with other European states and the dispatch of scholars to foreign centers of learning; he forecast the founding of large industrial enterprises; he sponsored religious toleration, which actually pleased no one. His views of the peasantry were most visionary of all; they included freedom of the serfs with land and the encouragement of colonization in new frontier areas. Attempts at such peasant programs came only in the nineteenth century. Surely Golitsin's vision was more far-sighted than Peter's, but he lacked the essentials of Peter's personality: the disregard of consequences, the confidence in his role, and the willingness to do violence to work his will.

Golitsin's domestic visions had little chance. The personal lives of Sophia and Golitsin were a scandal and their Polish manner of life offended the boyars and clergy, who accused them of sympathizing with Catholicism. It was natural that Old Believers, church leaders, *streltsi,* and, in fact, all traditionalists, should lean more and more to the inactive Natalia Naryshkin, who was forced to take no stand on anything but whose court radiated comfortable conservatism. All of Golitsin's visions of domestic reform would have to await the winning of power; the reforms would be the product of his victory and not the route to it. That route was along the traditional lines of the century —military glory and conquest.

Golitsin and Sophia registered two outstanding achievements in foreign affairs, both designed to win glory and promote their claims to the throne in their own right. It was the tragedy of the Regency that, of these accomplishments, one was useless because it was unknown in its effects, and the other because it was only too well known in its temporarily disastrous consequences. The first was the Treaty of Nerchinsk with China, the second was the Holy League with Poland.

The Treaty of Nerchinsk, ratified in 1689, was the first pact signed by the Chinese Empire with a European power. Its terms, negotiated by Jesuit intermediaries on the River Amur, confirmed the claims of Muscovite explorations to the Pacific. Acceptance of the Amur as the boundary opened Russia's eastern frontiers to the Pacific and beyond. The Treaty also established the right of Muscovy to diplomatic and commercial representation in the Chinese capital. Yet this opening between two vast empires was of no political benefit to Sophia and her lover, for it was of no concern to the Muscovites, whose vision of their homeland could hardly encompass the Pacific in 1905, much less in 1689. It was also true that the Treaty came in the waning days of the Regency.

The Holy League with the Poles was quite different. The Perpetual Peace which Golitsin signed with Jan Sobieski of Poland in 1686 was only too well known. The King of Poland had been busy since 1683 in forming a league to eject the Turk from Europe. To safeguard his eastern front Sobieski was willing to make final the armistice of Andrusovo of 1667 and to give Muscovy permanent title to the city of Kiev. Sophia and Golitsin were able to boast that they had made fast to Muscovy all the lands east of the River Dnieper and the ancient capital on its right bank, that they had completed the work of Romanov reconquest and wrested from the Poles permanent recognition of Muscovy's existence and rights. But Sophia and Golitsin were not content with that achievement and listened with interest to Sobieski's further proposals for active Muscovite aid against the Turks. Advice against such a Polish alliance came from every quarter: Church leaders and the populace saw it as treason to Orthodoxy to mix with the ancient enemy; the Hetman of Ukraine warned that failure would bring the Turks and their Tatar allies into the heart of Ukraine; General Gordon, the Scots general in Muscovite service since 1665, spoke of the difficult logistics of such a war; and close advisors warned of the dangers of a reaction at home if such a campaign should go awry. But nothing would deter the Regent and her aspiring Tsar —they would ride to power in their own names on the strength of a great Orthodox victory over the infidel.

The Polish alliance was indeed a major event in Russian history. It signified the conclusion of the reconquest, for the Swedes had already recognized the permanent rights of the Romanovs over their territories and now the obstinate Poles had done the same. More than that, this treaty of 1686 was the first major break in the ranks of Muscovy's enemies and the opportunity for Muscovy to attack one of the trio of frontier adversaries without invoking the counterattack of the others. Thus, Muscovy passed from defensive to offensive foreign policy in league with like-minded European monarchs. From this path there was to be no return, and in it was prefigured Peter's alliance with the northern powers against Sweden. For Sophia and Golitsin, of course, there was a more proximate concern: Would the military campaigns to which they had committed Muscovy be successful? Their futures depended upon the answer.

Golitsin took personal command and aimed his campaign at the Crimea, thinking to humble those ancient marauders of the Muscovite frontier, the Crim Tatars, and then to defeat their Turkish patrons in their Crimean fortresses. The progress of the army of 100,000 was extremely slow and morale was very poor: the nobles had no interest in supporting Golitsin's ambitions, the *streltsi* longed for their prosperous shops and political bases in congenial Moscow, and the conscripted serfs had no idea of where they were or why. The Tatars set the tall feather grass of the steppes afire and threw the Muscovite columns into panic. Golitsin and his army, within 130 miles of the Isthmus of Perekop, turned back in disarray.

Blame for the failure was heaped upon the Hetman Samoilovich of Ukraine for his alleged incompetence, and Golitsin chose his own man, Ivan Mazepa, as the new Hetman. Golitsin then made one more attempt to recoup his losses with a second Crimean campaign in 1689. After three months his army reached the Isthmus, already much harassed by the mobile cavalry of the Crim Tatars. The Turks garrisoned the Crimean fortresses at will from the sea and repulsed the desultory attacks of the Muscovites and inflicted heavy losses on them. Twenty thousand Muscovites were killed, 15,000 captured, and the rest retreated. Sophia, who had envisioned a coronation at the end of the campaign, had now to make other plans as the extent of the disaster was spread throughout Muscovy by the unhappy survivors in the last months of 1689. The failure of two military campaigns undertaken to win the throne might legitimately be expected to lose it.

While Sophia and Golitsin were working out their destiny between 1682 and 1689, Peter, supposedly co-Tsar with his half-brother Ivan, actually lived in a kind of semi-exile with his mother Natalia in the village of Preobrazhenskoe. This little town, twenty miles from Moscow on the banks of the River Yauza, had been a favorite country residence of the Tsar Alexei. Prince Kurakin, premier diarist of the age and an admirer of Sophia, testified that Natalia and her entourage lived on the kindly charity of the Regent. Actually, Natalia constantly begged funds from friendly sources, including the Patriarch, the monks of the Trinity Monastery, and even the Metropolitan of Rostov. From the very beginning, Preobrazhenskoe was tagged as the center of the traditionalists, and its role as a refuge for those disaffected from the Regency grew with each passing year.

Peter was ten years old when his family was deposited in Preobrazhenskoe. Although his half-brothers and sisters had been educated by the distinguished scholar Polotsky, Peter from age three had been in the hands of a tutor named Nikita Zotov, a clerk in a government office and a total alcoholic. At Preobrazhenskoe Peter abandoned all pretense at formal education; he was as much estranged from the dark wailings and recriminations of his mother's shadowy court as he was from the sophisticated style of Sophia's court in Moscow. His formal duties, appearances at public receptions in the Kremlin, were few and far between. For most of the years between 1682 and 1689 Peter was being taught in schools hardly normal for a Tsar of Muscovy.

While co-Tsar Ivan in the Kremlin was bound by the rituals of his office, Peter was free to roam the countryside and pursue his own interests. To the annoyance of his ambitious mother, Peter easily eluded his tutors, played constantly in the outdoors, and searched out his own companions. Physically powerful, natively intelligent, and immensely curious, Peter learned to sail a boat, operate a forge, survey a field, build fortifications and blast them down, fire artillery, drink like a trooper, and carouse with the ladies. Many of these skills, and most especially the last two, Peter acquired from his attachment to the Foreign Quarter.

The Foreign Quarter was the suburb where Tsar Alexei had required that foreign merchants and soldiers make their homes so as not to contaminate the Muscovites with their habits and heresies. Situated between Preobrazhenskoe and Moscow, it was inevitable that Peter should have been attracted by its neat homes, scoured streets, air of gaiety, technical marvels, and the sophisticated gentlemen who dwelt there. Franz Lefort, a Swiss adventurer in Russian service since 1675, became his dearest friend and adviser. Peter spent many a long night drinking among the riotous infidels in the tavern of the Dutchman Mons. Here he first saw the skills and marvels which stocked his dreams. Here General Patrick Gordon, veteran of both Golitsin campaigns, taught him strategy. Here Timmerman and Zommer taught him geometry, artillery, and sailing. And here also Peter found his first mistress, Anna Mons, the daughter of the innkeeper.

At Preobrazhenskoe Peter began to exercise his practical nature and growing fund of knowledge acquired in the Foreign Quarter in peculiar forms of "play." In 1683 he began to organize the "toy regiments" (*poteshnye*), staffing them with young men of high and low degree. Some were sent from Moscow to humor the young Tsar, while others Peter found in the streets of the towns. From the latter group came Alexander Menshikov, origin unknown or, if we are to believe Prince Kurakin, "by birth lower than a Pole," who became drinking companion to the Tsar and ultimately the richest man in Russia. The Ordnance Office of the Kremlin was forever receiving orders from Peter for equipment and uniforms. His two toy regiments, the Preobrazhensky and the Semenovsky, named for a nearby village, were officered by willing foreigners. Full-scale battles involving real artillery rattled the quiet afternoons of the Tsaritsa Natalia. A model fortress called Pressburg was built for these maneuvers and Peter learned to play the drum for the mock attacks. Soon the Tsar was even building small ships on the banks of Lake Periaslavl.

This military play had its significant aspects, although neither Natalia nor Sophia could see much but the boisterous pranks of an undisciplined child who forecast no political future for himself. The Guards Regiments as the core of the new Imperial Army had their beginnings here. Also, Peter bound the foreign soldiers closely to himself; no Muscovite Tsar had ever commanded the personal affections of the foreigners as Peter did nor shown them how well they might prosper under his patronage. Finally, these years prefigured the personal nature of Peter's authority and the extension of that authority to men pushed by his will to high places in the state over and against the ancient aristocracy. The "fledglings," or favorites of Peter, emerged in the Preobrazhenskoe period, men of provincial or foreign or obscure backgrounds who would have expected little advancement in Muscovy. They tied themselves to Peter's future and for their loyalty they would be amply rewarded.

The Tsaritsa Natalia did not bear the behavior of her son with equanimity. He played at war and roistered with the foreigners while the bitterness of Muscovite politics grew steadily more intense. The scene in Alexei Tolstoi's novel *Peter the First* rings true, when one of Natalia's servants sent in search of the young Tsar kneels in the dust at the gate of the Foreign Quarter begging Peter to come home, fearful to enter the mysterious precincts and fearful to return to the rage of the powerless mother. Natalia chose a mother's eternal solution for a roving son; surely the tranquillity of married life would calm the young man and return him to his duties. Peter was wed in

1689 to a drab and traditional young wife, Eudoxia Lopukhin, the daughter of a court officer. Eudoxia contributed little to her husband except a son, Alexei, whose fate would be a national tragedy. Peter spent two months with his wife and then hurried back to his outdoor games.

Peter, seventeen in 1689, was still cut off from the main business of his realm; of the problems of Muscovite society he knew little and seemed to care less. Natalia gauged her son accurately in those days and, seeing in him no disposition to act for himself in this time of opportunity, decided to act for him. The failure of the second Crimean campaign in 1689 was the signal for action. The *streltsi* especially, upon whom Sophia now leaned more heavily than ever, were in an uproar over the prolonged service demanded of them in distant climes for which they reaped no reward except defeat. In August, 1689, Sophia was either calling out the *streltsi* for normal escort duty or else was moving against Preobrazhenskoe before it could move against her. Whatever the truth, it was surely in Natalia's interest to have rumors spread rapidly that Sophia was attempting to murder the co-Tsar. Peter was awakened in the dead of the night and whisked away on horseback, numb with terror, to the friendly and impregnable walls of the Troitsa Monastery. Some historians maintain that the peculiar spasms which contorted Peter in moments of exceptional stress dated from this midnight flight.

From the security of Troitsa Natalia issued a call in her son's name for all loyal Muscovites to rush to the aid of their beleaguered Tsar. Slowly the *streltsi* and merchants of Moscow, wearied of the burdens of active government and war, slipped from the city and drifted towards Troitsa. The Patriarch, always close to Natalia, made his open break with the regime for public effect. The foreign mercenaries under General Gordon, tightly bound in Peter's friendship, tested the wind, found it blowing towards Troitsa, and marched to join their new leader; Gordon called his defection from the Regency "the decisive break." Sophia watched the disintegration of her party and knew that her day was done. Peter assumed power under the guidance of his mother on September 22, 1689. Vasili Golitsin was stripped of his estates and exiled, Sophia was forcibly retired to a convent where she dwelt until her death in 1704, and the innocuous co-Tsar Ivan V was allowed to retain his title until his own natural death in 1696.

Yet the year 1689 does not date Peter's real accession to power. He was quite content to leave government in the hands of his mother and her cronies. From 1689 to Natalia's death in 1694, therefore, Muscovy was governed by Natalia, her brother Lev Naryshkin, and the Patriarchs Joakhim (died 1690) and Adrian. Prince Kurakin called these years "a time of wholesale corruption and state theft," and Natalia "a woman of poor intelligence, incapable of governing." Contrary to the visions usually conjured up by the name of Peter the Great, the first years of government by Peter's party were corrupt, rife with injustice, sodden with religiosity, shot through with parochialism, and dominated by hatred of everything foreign. No drive for high principle lighted any corner of this government by faction.

Peter in these years showed no promise, and the appeals of his subjects to repair the ravages to his people went unheard. He was far more interested in pursuing his military games, feasting constantly in the Foreign Quarter, and enlarging his regiments with what his mother chose to call, in terms reminiscent of Sara Roosevelt's description of her son's political colleagues, "vagabonds and vagrants, butlers and attendants." The Tsar spent all of 1691 in maneuvers, most of 1692 with his Dutch ship carpenters on Lake Periaslavl, and part of 1693 relishing his first taste of the salt sea at Archangel. In 1694 he engineered a great series of military games at Kozhukhovo, just outside Moscow, in which 30,000 troops were engaged over a three-week period. Special works were built and government clerks and townsmen were ordered to participate to fill out the formations. In the course of these games twenty-four died and fifteen were wounded. It was significant that the mock battles occurred close to Moscow so that the population could view them, and significant also that *streltsi* and the toy regiments were hurled against one another and that the *streltsi* were programmed to lose. The defeated *streltsi* were then paraded through Moscow in a ceremony foreshadowing their final degradation five years later.

When Natalia died in 1694 Peter was already a full-grown specimen of great strength, six feet eight inches in height and weighing about 230 pounds. He had a roving and curious mind and a savage if sporadic temper; he was constantly carousing or working; he loved crafts and sought to master every one; he hated ceremonial and it was common knowledge that "the Tsar cannot stomach a large dwelling"; he was loyal to friends to a fault and given to sentimental displays toward the great and the lowly. He had an outrageous sense of humor, institutionalized in its most pleasant form in the hidden fountains of Peterhof which still attack the unwary tourist. Fireworks were his passion and no event was properly celebrated without them even at the constant cost of life and limb. Drinking was his primary sport but never a seriously debilitating one; he could drink from night to morn without apparent ill effect and would rouse exhausted advisers to their work at the normal hour. He was prone to use his fists on stupidity and resistance, and Alexander Menshikov, himself no light-weight, was a favorite and deserving target.

Peter's personal traits were put on public display in strange form in these years. The Tsar and his comrades formed a group called the "Most Drunken Assembly of Fools and Jesters," dedicated to drinking and carousing in their most violent forms. The carousing was a vulgar parody of the Orthodox clergy, with Nikita Zotov, the ancient drunk-ard, as Prince-Pope, Romodanovsky as All-Jesting Patriarch, and every-one else with a churchly rank. This group when properly lubricated would stage night parades through the staid streets of Moscow, with Bacchus portrayed by Nikita Zotov, stark naked and crowned with laurel leaves, escorted by Peter beating a tattoo on his drum. Is there any wonder, then, that Muscovites saw little to hope for in their young Tsar and much to fear? Some historians have read a deep resentment of the Orthodox Church into these displays and a forecast of Peter's handling of the Church. They hardly represented so well-developed an attitude, but did indicate a strong strain of anticlericalism, a feel-ing that ignorant priests had too much to say about the business of state. These exhibitions did the image of the Tsar no good and much harm, and, added to later evidence, helped to convince his subjects in large numbers that they were dealing with a maniac at best and the Antichrist at the very worst.

When Natalia died in 1694, therefore, the emptiness of the Musco-vite monarchy was clearly exposed. Peter could either leave that monarchy to the crude ministrations of the greedy and corrupt func-tionaries whom his mother had gathered around the state trough, or he could pick up its scepter which Sophia had at least begun to burnish anew. It was not nearly so clear as the future history of his reign would lead one to believe that Peter would choose to lift that scepter. Two major events were instrumental in shaping his emer-gence to real power: the military campaign against the Turkish for-tress of Azov and the Grand Embassy to western Europe. These two advanced schools provided the young ruler with the only kind of education which ever meant much to him—practical confrontation with tough experience. At the same time, these two undertakings forecast the central themes of Peter's reign: reorganization for incessant war and the emerging presence of Russia in European politics.

There has been criticism of Peter's campaigns southward against the Turks in the wake of Golitsin's defeats as wasted effort in difficult and unrewarding areas while Muscovy's true interest lay on the Baltic coast. The criticism is unjust for a variety of reasons. Peter was largely concerned with the perfection of his military instruments, and consequently the example of his ancestors was his guide. The seventeenth century had identified three enemies, Poland, Sweden, and Turkey, who contested Muscovite frontiers and blockaded its routes to world commerce; but hitherto an attack on one was likely to produce a reaction in all three. Only in Peter's time had the Holy League definitively isolated Turkey. Peter made only one change in the Golitsin program, choosing the river routes to Azov rather than the land routes to Crimea. For Peter the Azov campaign was a continuation of his maneuvers, providing a fortification to test his army with the greatest possibility of success and the minimum possibility of severe consequences in case of defeat, since even the failures of Golitsin had not brought the Turks or Tatars to Moscow. This would not have been true of a western campaign at this time; if Peter had opted so early to make war on the Swedish Baltic he might well have invited the end of his state as well as the end of his reign.

It should also be recalled that Muscovy was still at war with the Ottoman Empire. The Turks had not taken Muscovy's attacks with good grace and had released the Crim Tatars for violent raids along the Ukrainian frontier. This demanded some response. At the same time, Golitsin's treaty commitments bore heavily on the Tsar; Peter suspected the Poles of seeking a separate peace, which would leave Muscovy to face the Turks alone, while the Poles were convinced that the change of Muscovite government foretold its withdrawal. Peter was persuaded by his advisers that he ought not to permit the Turks to end their isolation at Muscovy's expense. Mazepa was also advising the young Tsar; the Hetman of Ukraine, installed in office through Muscovite intervention, was shaky in his post and fearful of internal plots and Tatar raids. He told Peter that the Zaporozhian and Don Cossacks were restless and believed that the inexperienced ruler in Moscow would not reassert Muscovite authority in the steppe. Mazepa therefore counseled a show of force in the south not only to frighten the Tsar's enemies but to pacify his subjects.

Franz Lefort also encouraged a campaign against Azov. The Swiss adventurer was planning to manage his protégé to glory, but that management would require a careful hand. Peter must visit the other great states of Europe, he must begin to play a role in their deliberations, he might even presume to take the natural place of the Muscovite Tsar at the head of a vast European coalition to expel the Turks from Europe. But Peter could not go as a beggar among the princes of Europe; the Tsar must carry with him the credentials of victory to ensure a proper reception and a respectful hearing. A victory at Azov would provide such credentials and bring Peter to the attention of his fellow monarchs as less a presumptuous stripling than a successful soldier-king. Lefort saw Azov as his opportunity: neither too hard nor too easy a labor for his untested Hercules to perform.

Peter's first campaign against Azov began in 1695. A large army was to move against the Turkish forts on the Dnieper in order to pacify the Cossacks and distract the Crim Tatars. The best troops would make the main assault on Azov: 30,000 men comprising the toy regiments, the troops of foreign discipline, and selected *streltsi*, divided into three contingents under Generals Gordon, Golovin, and Lefort. There was no supreme commander and the decisions of the three generals were subject to Peter's review. The Tsar considered himself too inexperienced to command and accompanied the armies as a loyal artilleryman of the Preobrazhensky Regiment, Bombadier Peter Alexeev. In June of 1695 the Muscovite troops approached the Turkish works at the mouth of the River Don.

Azov might have been far from the great fortresses of the Rhineland, but it was substantial enough to test the mettle of Muscovy. The fortifications stood ten miles upstream from the Sea of Azov on the left bank of the Don. Just above the main fort two towers stretched an iron chain across the river to bar the passage of ships past the forts. Siege works were begun but the essential weakness of the expedition was quickly revealed; a convoy of eighteen Turkish supply ships arrived to provision the fortress and the Muscovites, without ships, were helpless to prevent it. Peter grew impatient, which was his most persistent weakness. The battle was unlike his early maneuvers, for the Tsar could not simply order the fall of the enemy's forts. Peter wanted action and General Gordon pleaded in vain against any rash storming tactics which would throw the whole expedition into jeopardy. On August 5 Peter ordered just such an operation and Gordon's predictions were painfully realized: the attack crumbled and 1,500 Muscovites died. Another assault failed miserably in September and

Peter, despite good news from his troops on the Dnieper, began a seven-week retreat toward Moscow. He must have thought often of Vasili Golitsin on that sad march.

Peter, in the wake of his first military action and first military defeat, revealed that quality of character so evident in the years to come; melancholy could exert no permanent power over him, for he had always a vibrant energy in reserve and he soon sought to make the best and learn the most from his adversity. Peter now knew that he needed siege engineers, and orders were issued to borrow them from the Austrians immediately. Army organization had been clumsy and Peter now recognized the need for a unified command. The campaign had suffered from poor transport and the idea of a canal system binding the steppe rivers together was also born in the aftermath of the Azov defeat. The Tsar similarly discovered the grave defects of his army: the *streltsi* and nobles were unwilling warriors far from home, and even the "toy regiments" had betrayed a need for more training. Finally, Peter discovered that Azov could be provisioned forever by sea while the Russians remained landlubbers. Muscovy must have a navy.

Peter retired to his headquarters at Voronezh, high up on the river Don, to reorganize for a second attempt at Azov. Voronezh awakened from its sleepy provincial life to find itself a booming microcosm of the Russia which was to come. A bustling industrial and military center sprang up at the Tsar's order to do one thing—put a Muscovite navy on the broad Don. To accomplish this task Peter began the first major galvanizing effort of his reign: foreign craftsmen were ordered to report to Voronezh, the province was commanded to provide 30,000 men for labor duty, and a Dutch galley was borne overland from Archangel to serve as a building model. In five months Peter and his Dutch carpenters built 23 armed galleys and 1,300 river boats. When the spring thaw came, Muscovy had its navy.

In May of 1696, as the second expedition departed for Azov, Peter's place in it signaled the change in Muscovite preparedness; the Tsar took proud command of an armed galley in his own fleet. Forty-six thousand Muscovites and 20,000 Cossacks laid down their siege works for the second time in early June. The day after they reached Azov the Muscovite ships broke the chain and sailed past the forts into the sea. A Turkish convoy of 20 supply ships arrived unescorted and seeing the Muscovites at sea, fled before them. Peter had won his first naval victory, modest but infinitely pleasurable. Austrian siege engineers

arrived in early July and Azov capitulated on July 19. Peter surveyed
the coast, ordered a naval base and harbor to be dredged at nearby
Taganrog, and commissioned appropriate celebrations. Victorious
Peter had become a soldier-king.

Peter assembled his *Boyar Duma* in October, 1696, to shape practical responses to the questions raised by his experiences at Azov. In
the decrees which were shaped in those meetings were prefigured the
larger projects of the Petrine reforms. War with the Turk was now
Peter's main business and war made demands. Decrees were issued
aimed at the creation of a permanent Muscovite navy of 50 ships on
the Black Sea: monasteries were to build and supply one ship for
every 8,000 serf households, nobles one ship for every 10,000 serf
households, and merchants 12 ships in all. The ships were to be ready
at Voronezh within eighteen months. Peter then ordered 3,000 infantry
transferred from Kazan to colonize Azov, with 3,000 *streltsi* detailed
to the same task to remind them of their miserable contribution to
the campaigns. The Tsar also decreed the conscription of a labor
force of 20,000 men from the towns of Ukraine to begin a Volga-Don
canal. In these meetings plans were made to send students abroad to
study engineering and military techniques, and 60 sons of the nobility
were so dispatched. The victorious Tsar's decrees to his advisers were
all examples of the ruler's autocratic will bent to the accomplishment
of a particular goal and in the process running roughshod over ancient
customs. The pattern of the Petrine reforms was set and the essential
outlines of the Petrine character revealed.

But if the Tsar was awakened to some of the practical requirements of his military ambitions and had decided to pursue them at
any cost to his subjects, that did not mean that he had decided to
truly govern the realm. Between 1694 and 1700 the Tsar planned
the campaigns, built the ships, and conscripted the men and supplies, but he ignored the daily problems of government administration and happily left them to drunkards, incompetents, and thieves.
The miserable administration which characterized the period of Natalia continued and intensified in the early years after her death.
Peter had not learned to love the details of government. The per-
secution of foreigners and foreign influence continued, hard as it
may be to reconcile such practices with the Petrine image. Church
prelates whose physical or intellectual roots were in the Kievan
Academy of Ukraine were removed from their posts and the Academy
in Moscow was purged. The inequitable tax system, the infamous

miscarriages of justice, the wholesale corruption in state offices, compounded by the emergency demands of the warrior Tsar for men, money, and supplies, were all intensifying the black mood of the Muscovite population. The Monk Avraam of the Troitsa Monastery dared to petition the Tsar in 1697 and to report the prevailing resentments of landlords and peasants alike: "The people moan and complain because of the failure of the one from whom they hoped so much; they thought that when the Great Sovereign grew up and married, he would abandon the frivolities of his youth and perform all things well. But become a man and married, the Tsar has turned to pleasure, leaving the good road and causing only sorrow and calamities."

The Tsar's response to these pleas was quite in the style of his fellow monarchs across Europe. Torture was liberally applied and many, including the brave Monk Avraam, were exiled. Tortures elicited a list of the most common complaints of the people: the continual presence of the Tsar in the Foreign Quarter where he dishonored himself before strangers, the punishment of true believers at Preobrazhenskoe, the abandonment of his wife, his menial labors in shipyards, the carousing parades, and the abandonment of the people to the extortions of vicious functionaries. The groans of the Muscovites were only beginning, they would grow more desperate as years went on, but even in these early days they found echoes in action. A plot was discovered in 1697 among the monks of the Andreyevsky Monastery to overthrow the Tsar and, just prior to Peter's departure for western Europe, one of the *diaki* of the *Duma* was accused of a similar plot. Five executions followed and the bodies allowed to hang rotting in Red Square as reminders of the fate of malcontents.

In the midst of this growing discontent Peter announced his intention to make a tour of western Europe. Historians have long debated the reasons for this unprecedented journey in 1697–98, but the debates have really been more over emphasis than interpretation. To revitalize the League against the Turks, to strengthen his navy, to enlist foreign aid for his military work—these seem sufficient for the times and for the character of the Tsar. To try to put these motives in some order of priority seems fruitless, for in the mind of Peter they were all bound together: he intended to carry on the war against the Turk and would need alliances and technical assistance to prosecute that war successfully.

Peter left Muscovy to travel abroad with a group of selected pupils, "for a monarch should feel ashamed to lag behind his subjects in any craft." Officially, Peter never left the Kremlin, for he traveled incognito as Cadet Peter Mikhailov. It was a bold move, perhaps even a foolish one, for the young ruler to depart his realm. No Tsar had ever passed the frontiers on such a journey and Peter's throne was not that secure; plots had been uncovered even in the week of his departure, the *streltsi* were rumbling over their treatment since the Azov campaigns, Sophia was no farther from another bid for power than a convent gate, and the popular reaction to his leaving was angry. Rumor held that the Tsar was taking his treasure to foreign lands, that he would convert to Protestantism or Catholicism, or that the Antichrist would return in his stead. Oblivious to all this ferment, Peter packed his bags for a journey which had beckoned him ever since his first encounter with the Foreign Quarter. Peter, it must be obvious by now, was a creature of supreme confidence.

The Grand Embassy left Moscow on March 20, 1697, for a journey of eighteen months. Two hundred and fifty officials and young nobles, the Tsar among them, were officially led by Franz Lefort. On the way to the Netherlands, the first major goal, Peter had two important meetings. The first of these came in Riga, still a Swedish port, where the incognito Tsar was handled a bit roughly by Swedish guards when he attempted to make an impromptu survey of the city's fortifications; Peter made no complaint at the time but mentioned it prominently three years later in his declaration of war on the Swedes. The second encounter came with Frederick III, Elector of Brandenburg and soon to be King in Prussia. Here he first heard mention of the vulnerability of the Swedes, although Peter had different projects on his mind and made no response to the suggestion.

Peter arrived in the Netherlands in August and made immediately for the town of Zaandam, the home of many of the Dutch carpenters whom he had known at Archangel and Voronezh. He spent only a week there, however, for public curiosity overwhelmed him and he traveled to Amsterdam to work in the privacy of the East India Company dockyards. Here Peter spent four months, and an English fellow worker observed that "the Tsar of Muscovy worked with his own hands as hard as any man in the yard." He wrote to the Patriarch Adrian to placate his fears that the Tsar dishonored himself by appearing as a common workman, explaining that he worked "not out of necessity, but to know the arts of the sea so that upon our return we may triumph over the enemies of Christ and become by His grace the liberator of Christians." But Peter tired of his Dutch sojourn, convinced that the Dutch system of naval architecture was largely one of improvisation, in the manner of a good cook who produces masterpieces with a dash of this and a slice of that, and therefore not sufficiently reducible to a method to be transferred to pupils in distant Muscovy.

Peter arrived in England in January, 1698. His incognito had slipped badly but he hardly bothered to preserve it. Deptford, a shipbuilding town, was his nominal headquarters for four months but he never really settled in. The Tsar observed Parliament, reviewed naval maneuvers with King William at Spithead, visited Windsor, the Mint, and the Royal Arsenal, and busied himself hiring craftsmen to come to Muscovy. Deptford, by the way, had its mementos of the Tsar. He rented the home of one John Evelyn and proceeded to demolish it with riotous living; the owner billed the government for damages which Christopher Wren estimated at £350.

Peter's next destination was Vienna, where he hoped to convince the Emperor Leopold to revitalize the League against the Turks. This task was hopeless since the government in Vienna, as those in Amsterdam and London, was too concerned that Louis XIV's claims to the throne of Spain were about to unleash a major war in the west. Peter planned a visit to Venice, where he hoped to learn about Mediterranean galleys and to find a more congenial reception for his Turkish plans from these traditional enemies of the Ottomans. But these plans were cut short by news in July that four *streltsi* regiments were in revolt.

Peter hastily departed the Austrian capital and made straight for Moscow. He must have wondered in those days whether his confident plan to leave his realm was not after all ill-conceived. Happily, he received news on the road that the *streltsi* revolt had been completely crushed. The Tsar stopped abruptly at Rawa in Poland and spent two pleasant weeks with Augustus II, "the Strong," of Saxony, the elected King of Poland. Peter and Augustus were soul mates; their drinking habits, their love of women, their physical size and stamina, all bound them together immediately. Peter noted that, of all the princes of Europe he had met, Augustus was surely the finest, and from Augustus he heard of the weakness of the Swedish Empire for the second time.

The Europeans among whom the Tsar traveled generally reacted favorably to the personality of the Tsar but most unfavorably to his princely character. The Electress of Hanover thought him a natural savage, with a "great vivacity of mind and a ready and just repartee. But with all the advantages with which nature had endowed him, it could be wished that his manners were a little less rustic. . . . If he had received a better education, he would be an accomplished man." Bishop Burnet in England thought him "a man of very hot temper, soon inflamed, and very brutal in his passions. . . . [He] seems destined by Nature rather to be a Ship Carpenter than a great Prince." The Austrian Ambassador in London was shocked that "all the time here he went about in sailor's clothing." A Swiss tourist was dismayed by the fact that "he has convulsions . . . I do not know from where it arises, but we must believe that it is a lack of good breeding." A Hungarian Cardinal thought him a nice enough fellow but "there is nothing in him which would distinguish him or declare him to be a Prince." In sum it seemed that he was congenial and curious but rough and uneducated. It was clear that a generation raised on the careful etiquette, the ceremonial and grandeur of Louis XIV, did not consider that Peter displayed any of the qualities of a proper monarch. This view reflects their limitations more than it does Peter's. Within a generation Europeans grown a bit weary of the trappings of majesty would find something strongly appealing in the practical and rustic Tsar.

Peter returned to Moscow in August of 1698 with an astonishing variety of people and things, including 300 craftsmen with 400 more to follow, tons of marble, stuffed animals, curios, and the latest tools and machines. The Tsar had even acquired a set of dental tools, and the Muscovite court henceforth lived in nervous expectation of a toothache. But he brought back with him also a new and broader vision of the possibilities of transformation, an esteem for the order, prosperity, and strength which prevailed among the Dutch and the English. He had seen two great powers of Europe in the process of formation and saw no reason why Muscovy should not be another.

The activities of the Tsar upon his return reflected both old resentments and new beginnings. He moved against the *streltsi*. An inquiry discovered that they considered their frontier service as a punishment and as an attempt to end their political role, and had spread rumors of the Tsar's death abroad and had propagandized widely for the return of Sophia. Those *streltsi* being sent to the frontiers had broken into open revolt in early June and had marched back upon the city of Moscow, but General Gordon and the Guards defeated them 50 miles from its gates. Peter seized the opportunity which he had sought since the riotous days of 1682 to purge the state of *streltsi* influence. The organization was completely destroyed and the way cleared for the new army. A secretary in the Austrian legation noted the executions at length in his diary and said of one of them that "three hundred and thirty who were all led out together to the axe's fatal stroke impurpled the plain far and wide with civil but impious blood. . . . The Tsar himself, sitting in his saddle, looked on with dry eyes at the whole tragedy, at this frightful butchery of a multitude of men, being only irate that several of the boyars had performed this unaccustomed task with trembling hands." Peter pressed his advantage to the maximum, implicating his half-sister Sophia in the plot and hanging a few of the *streltsi* on her convent wall as a gentle reminder to her of the difficulties of political life. He implicated his innocent wife Eudoxia as well and secured a divorce and her incarceration in a convent. The *streltsi* revolt had indeed been useful: at one stroke it freed Peter from a national threat and a domestic encumbrance.

Muscovites could not help but notice the strange behavior of their Tsar upon his return. It was quickly known in the city that Peter did not visit the Kremlin to venerate the icons and give thanks to God for his safe return nor did he visit his patient wife and son, but rather streaked straight for the drunkards of the Foreign Quarter and the arms of his mistress, Anna Mons. The very next day, at a public reception to celebrate the Tsar's return, he went about the court cutting the beards and trimming the long robes of his advisers. Within the week decrees appeared on these matters: beards were to be cut or subjected to taxes that descended in severity from noble to peasant, and the same rules applied to the customary Muscovite dress. Peter now insisted that a people in the process of moving into the modern world ought to look the part. Peter also decreed a change from the Muscovite to the Julian calendar to take place in December, 1699. The New Year was to be celebrated on January 1 rather than in September, and proper festivities were ordered. "And to celebrate this new undertaking and this new century, the following is ordered. . . . Let reputable citizens arrange decorations of pine, fir, and juniper boughs along the busiest streets and by the houses of eminent church and civil persons. . . . Poorer persons should place at least one bough on their gates." Peter went on to instruct all his subjects to exchange joyous greetings and to fire guns and rockets. There is something frighteningly modern about an autocracy which considers it within its power to order people to be happy.

It is a temptation to play down the social changes of 1699–1700 as being surface and superficial, motivated largely by the Tsar's impatience on his return from Holland and England to see something of the neatness and order which characterized those societies. But such a view would ignore the primary role of the external in Muscovite life, the overwhelming devotion to the appearance of things and the deep emotional attachment which the outward signs of life commanded. Those who recall the Great Schism produced by the Nikonian reforms will not underestimate the impact of these Petrine social decrees. Beards were sacred, the sign of man's spiritual estate worn by Christ and his saints; to be brought before God on the Day of Judgment without one's beard was a fearsome thought and even "fledglings" close to the Tsar hid their shorn whiskers that they might be buried with them. Muscovite dress was the sign of God's holy people, constant from generation to generation. Who could bear to see the body and the robes defiled to please the foreigners? Who could bear a new calendar in which the Tsar presumed to dictate to God how the days of life were to be numbered and which took as its model the schemings of Rome? And who could happily celebrate in the style of heretical nations? These simple changes so cavalierly ordered by the Tsar, which modern readers may consider simple or even ridiculous, were deeply disturbing to those upon whom they were laid. They generated, as a matter of fact, far more resistance than the more substantial but more subtle Petrine reforms which might have passed more easily had the forms of national life been left unchallenged. The early nineteenth-century historian Karamzin felt that such attacks on the customary lives of the people were cruel, unusual, and unnecessary. Let us say in Peter's defense that he may have felt that the Muscovite world view would have to change before changes imposed upon it could take root. If so, he had a point.

Peter's travels and the radical social innovations undertaken at his return struck hardest at and elicited most response from the Old Believers, who were already deeply suspicious of the state which had condemned their faith. For them the change of calendar was a diabolic device to hide the fact that the year of Anti-christ had come. Rumors spread that the real Tsar was a prisoner in some foreign land and that the returning Tsar was an impostor placed by the Protestants to destroy the true faith. Others whispered that the Tsar was a changeling, substituted for in the cradle by a son of Nikon or of Franz Lefort. Surely the reason for Peter's failure to visit the churches on his return was that God had prevented this evil substitute from setting foot in the holy places, and the failure of the Tsar to visit his wife, followed by his divorce, simply proved that Eudoxia would not have recognized him as the true Tsar and would have revealed his imposture. Previous resentments against a frivolous Tsar were now being transformed into a deep fear of the Tsardom. And so the Grand Embassy and its immediate consequences were indeed important, since they served to follow the religious cleavage of the Nikonian reform with a political and social one, and to divide the lower classes of Muscovy even more from the state which claimed to rule for their welfare.

By 1700, much had happened in Muscovy. Peter slowly but surely accepted the burdens of Muscovite responsibility: he became a soldier-king who had won his first victory against the Turks and had begun the galvanization of his state's resources for major offensive war; he had become a European diplomat, accustoming Europe to the reality and the presence of Muscovites; he had become a social reformer, shaping his people by force into an image which would assist the release of their potential for innovation, and had thereby aroused serious rumblings of resistance to his will. He had come closer than his predecessors to being an absolute ruler, for the *streltsi* had been destroyed and the army was now the Tsar's army. All these beginnings were now to be tested and expanded in twenty years of war.

❋ 3 ❋

The Great Northern War

The monarchs of seventeenth- and eighteenth-century Europe scrupulously obeyed the injunction of Machiavelli that a prince should take up for his exclusive study the making of war. War was indeed the primary occupation of these monarchs both "pragmatic" and "enlightened" in the early modern era, although they were as careful as their successors in the nineteenth and twentieth centuries to cloak their combat in terms of moral necessity. The glory and progress of the state were viewed as largely and simply a problem of foreign policy, and few if any rulers of this age were deeply involved with the welfare of their subjects beyond their capacity as taxpayers and conscripts. Peter was no exception, and the years of his reign were years of constant war.

Since Peter the Great was essentially a soldier it has often been treated as a charge against him that all of his reforms were the product of his wars and were therefore haphazard in their origins and unforeseen in their consequences. That this emerges as an indictment stems from a preoccupation with comparisons of the Petrine reforms with twentieth-century developments, to the neglect of comparing Peter's work with that of his fellow European monarchs. Wherever these monarchs of the early modern era aspired to centralize their states, to destroy the forces of internal opposition, to arrogate absolute power to the crown, and to protect themselves from their like-minded rivals, they found the army the traditional and the most logical instrument with which to work their will. The French army, for example, underwent a significant seventeenth-century renovation in response to incessant war and naturally stimulated reforms of Richelieu and the

Sun King. The drive of the Prussian Grand Elector to build the first
standing army in the Germanies also demanded changes in taxation,
administration, and social structure. An army which was permanent,
modern, and responsive solely to the monarch's will would serve as
the primary force in unifying the population, repressing internal resistance, and protecting and expanding the glory of the state. All this
is simply to say that if the making of war and the reform of the army
were central to the Petrine reforms, so were they also central to the
reorganization of France, Prussia, and other European states. There is
little point in bringing a charge against Peter that he was a monarch
of his age. Those states which waged war longest and with some
success were the states in which the reforms associated with the centralizing absolute monarchy were undertaken with the greatest vigor.
One may regret that Peter the Great was neither a prophet nor a
philosopher on the throne, but prophets and philosophers were singu-
larly hard to come by on any throne even in that most enlightened of
centuries.

Peter as the premier soldier of Muscovy was forced to the realization, as were most of his royal colleagues across Europe, that the old
sanctions of authority and the old relationships between states were
being transformed, that those who valued internal unity and external
strength had better seize and direct the trend toward a strong military
establishment and find support for that establishment in the administrative, technical, and commercial developments of the age. Peter
had begun to learn these lessons in the *streltsi* revolts and at Azov,
as Louis XIV had learned them in the *frondes* and in the War of
Devolution. Such administrative, technical, and economic foundations
were as yet only beginning to develop in Muscovy at Peter's accession,
and they remained rudimentary in many European areas long after
Peter had passed away. Peter came to a knowledge of his needs and
of the vast social reorganization required to fulfill them only very
slowly, for only very slowly did he learn to rule and to fight.

Peter, especially in the years between 1700 and 1709, was a soldier
driven to concern himself with the immediate requirements of a
"modern" war. In the long process of delivering himself of these concerns he would evolve a broader vision of his work. Peter was a
practical man who learned his lessons from experience; his original
experience of total war with Sweden was desperate and therefore
called forth desperate measures. But those measures and their consequences were in themselves a school of experience and in turn led

him to consider in more tranquil times the organization and direction of his work.

The early years of the Great Northern War with Sweden were plagued by defeats and threats of invasion, and Peter's reactions were necessarily spasmodic and hand-to-mouth. This is not to say that Peter's imagination went uninspired by the image of an ordered and prosperous society called up by the Foreign Quarter and by western Europe, but only that in the first decade of the Northern War Peter had little time to coordinate his distant dreams with the daily requirements of the battlefield which engulfed him. One decision of the Tsar in the field led inevitably to a hundred others. Money, for example, was a constant necessity, but money implied new taxes, taxes implied a census, a census required census takers, and census takers meant at least minimum literacy; schools, in turn, required books and teachers, which, of course, required more money. The reader can perform the exercise for himself, starting with any obvious war requirement and deducing its necessary foundations. Is it artillery? Then where are the mines, the forges, the managers, the skilled workers, and the transport system which will produce and finally deliver those guns to the army at the front? Thus, the first years of the Northern War produced a mass of edicts and requirements which Peter in later years, especially after the victory at Poltava in 1709, would have to clarify, refine, and reorganize. Regardless of the fact, therefore, that Peter's contact with the Foreign Quarter, his travels in Europe, and his social reforms of 1698–99 indicate a more coherent vision of his tasks than many historians have been willing to concede to the "artisan Tsar," war was still the central force in releasing the reforms and channeling their directions.

Peter's approach to the main occupation of his reign, the Great Northern War, was indeed cavalier. Peter had no idea of a war in the north until 1698 and even then it was but a suggestion made to him in passing during his European journey. Everything that the Tsar had undertaken in fortification, supply, shipbuilding, transport, and reinforcement had been concentrated southward against the Turk until well into 1699. It seems astonishing and certainly revealing of the nature of the reforms to come that for a war with Sweden which lasted twenty-one years, Peter made less than four months of real preparation.

The shaping of a new direction for Peter's military activity was a many-sided affair. Strongly involved was the disintegration of the

European Holy League against the Turk. Peter had been disappointed during the Grand Embassy in his attempt to revitalize the coalition for the expulsion of the Turks from Europe; the European powers were too agitated by the plans of Louis XIV which were about to erupt in the War of the Spanish Succession. Peter had left an ambassador at the peace talks then underway with the Turks at Carlowitz on the Danube. Austria rushed to a decent peace while Peter's demands produced only a two-year truce between Muscovy and the Turk to discuss the terms. Peter had been abandoned by his allies and his resentment of Austria's perfidy was strong.

Peter's first ambassador to the Ottoman Porte was transported past Kerch by the Voronezh fleet in a fine display of ships and barges designed to impress the Turks with the wonder of Muscovites with sea legs. The negotiators met from November of 1699 to June of 1700. Peter's demands were originally extensive: annexation of all the forts he had taken, the right of Russian commercial vessels to sail the Black Sea, renunciation of tribute payments which had not been paid to the Crim Tatar for a decade, guarantee of no further Tatar raids against Muscovite territory, and the return of the Holy Sepulchre to the custody of the Orthodox Church; in this last can be traced the origins of later Russian claims to protect Orthodox Christians under Ottoman rule. All of these demands, however, were dropped or moderated in 1700. The Turks, never happy to negotiate a permanent peace with their Orthodox enemy, arranged a thirty-year truce which destroyed the Dnieper forts but returned their sites to the Turk, let Peter keep Azov, gave the Muscovites representation at Constantinople, and guaranteed rights of Muscovite pilgrimage to the Holy Land. The truce was signed in July, 1700. Meanwhile, other forces had come into play.

Realization that Muscovy could not revitalize the League against the Turk was accompanied by recommendations from new sources for the redirection of Peter's policy. The sources of these recommendations were Frederick William of Prussia and Augustus II, Elector of Saxony and King of Poland, who combined to urge Peter to join them in the partition of Sweden. Peter on his European journey had only half listened to such proposals, for his friendship with the Swedes was strong and they had even sent 300 cannon for his use in the Turkish war. But with the growing drift to peace with the Turk, Peter was faced with the generally accepted fact in northern Europe: the weakness of Sweden and the clear intent of its neighbors to take advantage of that weakness. Peter would have been a ruler of a different century to have ignored the temptation.

Sweden indeed seemed to her neighbors to be on the verge of collapse. The age of Sweden as a great power, dating from its German intervention under Gustavus Adolphus a century before, was coming to an end. The provinces of the Swedish empire collected in that century seemed bloated and overripe, ready to be shaken off and collected by adventurous neighbors. Those provinces which had made the Baltic a Swedish lake—Schleswig, Pomerania, Livonia, Ingria, Karelia, and Finland among them—were too tempting for the powers of the north to resist. At the same time, the preoccupation of France with a grand coalition forming against it withdrew its protection of Swedish interests. Most tempting of all was the reputation of the Swedish monarch; Charles XII, born in 1682 and thus ten years Peter's junior, was considered by all of Europe to be peculiar, weak, and unworthy.

At the center of the conspiracy against Sweden was Augustus II, Elector of Saxony and elected King of Poland. Augustus was nicknamed "the Strong" as much for his 168 illegitimate children as for his size and strength. His policy was purely dynastic, and he diligently searched the provinces of the north for royal homes for the numerous children of the Saxon house. Although Augustus intended to utilize his Polish subjects for a Swedish war, it was in expectation that the conquest of Courland and Livonia would provide fat new limbs for his family tree. The tool of his ambition was a Livonian landlord named Johan Reinhold Patkul, who came into his service in 1699. Patkul was an inveterate enemy of the Swedish crown, representing those German landlords of the Baltic coast who had been dispossessed by the Swedes. Wandering and landless, he was prepared to offer to Augustus II the loyalty and help of the Baltic nobility against the Swedish occupation. Augustus sent Patkul to Peter to urge an alliance against the Swede, and this time Peter, on the verge of a Turkish peace, listened attentively.

The coalition which formed in 1699 was one fraught from its origins with difficulties and indecision. Only Denmark was ready for an unqualified commitment. Brandenburg, wavering between its interests in eastern and western Europe, finally opted for the coalition against Louis XIV. Poland was a great problem, since Augustus, as Polish King, could not put the question of a Swedish war before the Polish Diet lest the debate warn the Swedes of his intentions and at the same time divide his own subjects. The use of Saxon troops in Poland would roil the Poles, and it required judicious bribes to permit Saxon troops to garrison themselves on the frontier of Swedish Livonia. Peter himself was not prepared for a quick decision. When he returned from an inspection tour of Azov, in October, 1699, he found two delegations awaiting him: the Swedes had arrived to renew their peace treaties of the seventeenth century, and Patkul and the Poles had come to propose the new alliance. Peter secretly accepted the new alliance but only on the condition that no Russian action would be forthcoming until a Turkish peace was assured, while publicly the Tsar reciprocated the peace overtures of the Swedes. Peter's rewards for his new alliance were to be the provinces of Ingria and Karelia on the Baltic.

It is fair to indict Peter for his hasty signing of this new alliance, even with the reservations he inserted. Too much is customarily made of Muscovy's ancient aspirations for a Baltic coastline and too little of the fact that Peter had ignored those aspirations until 1699 when European conditions drew his attention to them. Every bit of the mobilization of his reign had thus far occurred in the south in expectation of a continued war against the Turk; no such work had even yet been contemplated in the bleak and inaccessible northern lands. At the same time, Peter considered his new allies to be substantial and resolved: they were not. He also considered Sweden too weak to resist and envisioned the coming war as an easy occupation campaign; it was not. He considered Muscovy ready for a confrontation with a recognized power after less than five years of building; it was not. Thus Peter's change of plans was hasty and ill-considered, hurried along by the flattering attention of northern monarchs. Peter was much too impressed by this new attention and much too willing to be bought into a common enterprise with them which would establish him as one of the new powers of the north. Peter admitted 24 years later, when such an admission could do him no harm but only enhance the memory of his accomplishment, that "Russia entered her war blindly, with no thought of her own weakness or the enemy's strength."

The war opened in January, 1700, as Augustus II launched his Saxon troops northward into Livonia and the King of Denmark attacked the neighboring territory of Holstein. The first months of war, as Peter awaited news of a peace with the Turk, went poorly for the allies. Augustus II had not concerted with the Livonian landlords and had been forced to retreat from Riga. August 18 was a fateful day: Peter received news of the Turkish truce and declared war on Sweden, alleging that he had been insulted by Swedish authorities when he passed Riga on the European Embassy. But on August 18 also, although Peter would not know it for some time, Charles XII had sailed boldly into the harbor of Copenhagen, his ferocious army escorted by the English fleet, and surgically removed Denmark from the war. So Peter blithely entered a war in which, unknown to him, one ally was in retreat and the other already defeated. It was the day when Muscovy unconsciously shifted from a peripheral role in a European coalition to the center of the northern European stage.

Peter launched his attack against the Swedish fortress of Narva in the province of Ingria. The Muscovite army of 35,000 men was badly trained, poorly equipped, and miserably led. The Tsar traveled in his usual place as a bombardier in the Preobrazhensky Regiment. Narva, with its garrison of a thousand men, required seven miles of Muscovite siege works to encompass it. Peter's army began its bombardment on October 31 and continued for two weeks, by which time the Muscovite artillery was blowing up its crews, ammunition was exhausted, the Swedes were making devastating sorties, and the misty marshlands were freezing under Muscovite feet. Things were bad for the Muscovites, but they would soon be worse.

Couriers pierced the frost-hard swamps in early November to tell the bombardier-Tsar that Denmark had fallen and that the much abused Charles XII, fast forcing reassessment of his military prowess, was on his way to Narva to handle the second member of the coalition in person. Nor was he alone; 18,000 seasoned Swedish soldiers, the muscle of Europe's premier army, were coming with him. Young Charles landed at Pernau and advanced along the coast. News of the coming of the Swedes spread among the shivering Muscovites, so lately peasants in the lands to the south, and now so far from home and miserable in these godforsaken climes; fearful rumors spread through the badly supplied camp, passed from ear to ear by men for whom the promise of battle brought neither memories nor thrills. In the midst of this dismal decline of morale and on the brink of the first serious test of his army, the Tsar mounted his horse and galloped for Novgorod.

There is much dispute about Peter's hasty departure. The worst version holds that Peter was overcome by the same panic which seized him on that fearful night in 1689 when he fled to Troitsa. The least convincing version holds that Peter left the field in order to avoid embarrassing his commander, the Duke de Croy. The most sympathetic interpretation, the one favored by Peter in later years, said that the Tsar foresaw the coming defeat and was hastening to the rear to erect fortifications, reorganize resources, and open contact with the Poles for the difficult days to come. Whatever the explanation, Peter did leave the field and only learned of the worst disaster of his reign at second hand from its survivors.

The Swedes appeared before Narva on November 30. For the reader accustomed to modern battles the fact that 18,000 Swedes had come on an exhausting trip across the winter Baltic to face twice their number of Muscovites might indicate a great Muscovite advantage; neither Muscovite nor Swede thought so. When the disciplined Swedish infantry burst out of a raging snowstorm upon the Muscovite works, the battle was over before a real engagement took place. The Russians fled their posts in panic, killing their foreign officers as they stampeded, and the Duke de Croy was speedier than the demands of honor would require to hand over his sword and extricate himself from this unseemly debacle. A Swedish soldier wrote from the field that "I have seen many a hard fought battle but never such a slaughter as that which befell the Muscovite hordes. The water in the trenches was turned to blood and the corpses were piled high in the bastions." King Charles, losing less than 2000 men, killed 5700 Muscovites, captured 10,000 prisoners, and seized the full Muscovite complement of 149 cannon. It was a sickening defeat by any European standard; for Peter it was the beginning of knowledge.

If Narva was a fateful battle, the decision of Charles XII in its wake was even more fateful. Although his staff strongly urged him to make his peace with Augustus and to march immediately upon Moscow, there to unseat a Tsar and proclaim Sophia or some other candidate, Charles would have none of it. His victories had inflated an already bulging ego: "the King thinks about nothing except war," wrote one of his generals; "he no longer troubles himself about the advice of others, and he seems to believe that God communicates directly to him what he should do." Charles chose to turn his back temporarily on the Muscovites and to hunt down the last of his presumptuous enemies, the King of Poland, in the heart of that kingdom. His decision was a mixture of tactic and imagination; he did not relish a march into the heart of Muscovy which would leave Augustus free to ravage his supply lines. At the same time, he had developed at

Narva a serious underestimation of Muscovite abilities which would cost him dearly in the future. He could leave their ruin until a later time "for there is no pleasure in fighting with the Russians, for they will not stand like other men but run away at once. . . . The best joke was when the Russians crammed onto the bridge and it broke under them. It was just like Pharaoh in the Red Sea. Everywhere you saw men and horses, their heads and legs sticking out of the water; our soldiers shot them like ducks." Charles, confident that the cowardly Russians could do nothing but await his return, turned into the lands of Poland to bring Augustus the Strong to judgment.

The effect of Narva on Peter was just as important. It was not in his nature to brood long while life was in him, and he soon dismissed the failure of his army as due to "inexperience." He knew that the decision of Charles XII to turn against Poland would grant him the most precious gift he could receive in these circumstances—time. "Time is like death," said Peter, "it pursues me everywhere." He had but a small supply of precious time to recoup the losses of Narva, to remedy inexperience, to restore morale, to resupply artillery; in short, to galvanize the resources of his state for a war which had been transformed from a promenade of imperial conquest into a vicious struggle for survival. Peter was too busy with rebuilding to permit himself the luxury of despair, and his memory in later years properly reflected his attitude after Narva: "That we lived through this disaster, or rather this good fortune, forced us to be industrious, energetic, and experienced."

The army had to be his primary concern and it is fruitless to look beyond it in these years immediately after Narva for the source of the reforms. The defense of Novgorod and Pskov against what seemed an imminent invasion was directed personally by Peter, and the Tsar himself toured the countryside rounding up the remains of his battered army to the extent of 20,000 men. He ordered Boris Golitsin to conscript another 80,000 troops, dispatched Anrius Vinius, his mining expert, to produce new artillery which numbered 300 pieces by the end of 1701, and decreed the conscription for melting of all church bells in north Russia. All of these activities represented the mobilization of a war state, a mobilization which the commitment to the coalition in 1700 had not forced but which the defeat at Narva made inevitable.

Peter between 1700 and 1709 produced an army of 100,000 men, but that figure does not tell the whole story. It required eleven conscrip-

tions based on the responsibility of specific provinces to furnish recruits for specific regiments to maintain the "immortal" Russian soldier
in the style of the ancient Persians. A cautious estimate holds that
100,000 men were lost and replaced in those years. Men were torn
from their homes on the formula of one recruit for every twenty peasant households; their enlistments were for twenty-five years and their
families did well to mutter the prayers for the dead and to speak of
those in Peter's army in the past tense, for few lucky enough to survive the battles could hope to survive the peacetime rigors of an
eighteenth-century army.

Men were useless without equipment and training; Peter had
learned that lesson at Narva. The production of muskets increased by
the thousands each year to an annual peak of 40,000 by 1711, and the
Demidov family earned the gratitude of their sovereign for the pro-
lific artillery production of the ironworks in the Urals. Textile factories
turned out uniform material to clothe the new army. Foreign mercenaries matched the men and the equipment with new training
methods in the Austrian, French, and Swedish manner, introducing
the bayonet and discipline to these new recruits.

It was to Peter's credit that he recognized immediately after Narva
that conscripting, equipping, and training his new army would require
time, and that the amount of time he could count upon was largely in
the hands of the mercurial King of Poland. So long as Augustus dashed
from pillar to post across the flat lands of Poland before his enraged
adversary, just so long could Peter build. The meeting of Peter and
Augustus at Dunaburg in 1701 was certainly a sad affair; two years
earlier these two giants presumptuously discussed the partition of
their neighbor; today they wondered how long they might maintain
themselves on their precarious thrones. Peter wanted the Poles to
join their King and his Saxons in the war, but the Poles, ever bargain-
ing in the shadow of disaster, asked for the return of Kiev. Augustus
ended by negotiating only for Saxony, and the Tsar promised him
20,000 men, 100,000 pounds of powder, 33,000 rubles a year for three
years, and 20,000 rubles to bribe the Polish Diet into action.

Poland was finally moved to take up the war of its King in 1704,
largely because it was too uncomfortable to ignore it. Charles had
been ravaging the countryside in pursuit of Augustus, making no
distinctions as to whose property he requisitioned. Yet even with a
declaration of war, the Poles were still terribly divided over its good
sense. Poland's declaration at least produced an unequivocal response

from Charles XII, who declared Augustus dethroned in July and had a Polish nobleman, Stanislas Lesczynski, named in his stead. The Swedish King also finally discovered the truth about his Saxon opponent—that Augustus cared not a whit how much of Poland was ravaged since he was but an elected visitor exploiting Poland for income and power. Having learned that, Charles turned into Saxony. The threat of desecration of his beloved Electorate brought Augustus to terms. He surrendered his kingship and his war at the peace of Altranstadt in 1706, and, for good measure, turned over Johan Reinhold Patkul to the avenging Swedish King. Charles dispatched Patkul in a vicious execution well worthy of the enlightened century.

News that his last ally had left the field called Peter to his main business and to the test of his work. The Tsar had been exercising his new army since 1701 by hacking down, slowly but methodically, the system of fortified Swedish posts along the Baltic coast. The remnant of the Muscovite army followed Charles into Ingria as the Swede passed the Duna and had cleared the province by the end of 1702 and begun the siege of posts in Livonia. In October, 1702, Peter joined his army for the attack on Noteburg on Lake Ladoga and renamed his conquest Schluesselburg. By May, 1703, Peter had moved 20,000 men to the Neva's mouth and laid the foundations of the Peter and Paul Fortress, the nucleus of his new city of Petersburg, and of a naval base in the estuary at Kronstadt. A Swedish fleet of nine ships tried to relieve the garrison and was captured by thirty galleys in Muscovy's first real naval victory. In August, 1704, Narva finally fell to the Muscovites. While all these small Swedish garrisons were slowly extinguished and the Baltic coast from Dorpat to Noteburg fell into Peter's hands, Charles pursued his elusive victory in Poland, assuring his worried aide: "Console yourself, dear Piper, the enemy will not drag the place away with them."

The news of the defeat of Augustus II ended Muscovite rejoicing. Whether the Baltic coastline accumulated since 1701 could be held now depended on the success of Peter's military transformation in these years. Peter believed that Charles XII would finally return to the Muscovite campaign and the Tsar was right. Peter ordered his troops into an orderly retreat from Grodno, intensified his fortifications, and awaited the climax.

That Charles XII would embark upon a Russian invasion was not as clear to Europe as it was to Peter. Charles now stood in Saxony with his grizzled soldiers, victorious in three kingdoms, pointed into western Europe at the crucial stage in the War of the Spanish Succession; both Louis XIV and his enemies wondered if Charles would now mingle the Northern War with the western one and throw his weight decisively for or against the Sun King. Such an intervention, reminiscent of that of Gustavus Adolphus, would certainly have cast Sweden again in a great European light. Both France and its enemies had emissaries at Altranstadt, and even the famed Duke of Marlborough arrived to convince the Swedish King to build his empire in the east. Muscovy was being used by Louis XIV and by his enemies to distract the new Alexander, and Peter sought their mediation in vain. Not for the last time was Russia being used by great powers for their advantage, as they urged Charles to seek his glory at Peter's expense.

Charles was also buoyed by rumors of serious troubles in Peter's realm. The popular reaction against the impositions of the war were finding concrete forms. Astrakhan had risen against its taxes and conscriptions in 1705–6, the Bashkirs of the Urals in the same years, and the Don Cossacks under Hetman Bulavin in 1707. The pressures of seven years of emergency demands were cracking the formal facade of Muscovy, and Peter was forced to pull regular army units from the line to pacify his subjects. Intelligence concerning these disturbances was reaching Charles by an avenue which we shall soon discuss. Fortunately for Peter, the worst of the revolts were over by 1708, too late for Charles to hear of it.

Finally, there was the determination of Charles XII—he was bent on his last mission. The coalition against him lay in ruins and kings had lost their crowns; only Peter remained, still picking away at Swedish property on the Baltic and, worst presumption of all, still on his throne. Charles was intent upon the Tsar's punishment, and a Swedish general reported that the King "believes that he is an agent of God on earth sent to punish every act of faithlessness." The emerging power of Muscovy was to be broken, Peter to be deposed, and Muscovy cradled again in its long sleep.

Charles XII passed the Vistula in January, 1708, leading his largest and toughest army. Forty-five thousand Swedes seemed aimed at the reoccupation of Livonia, but reports indicated that its lands had been so devastated by Muscovite campaigns that it could not support the army. Then Charles ignored Peter and his Muscovites, who waited less than a hundred miles away in fortified Smolensk. He studied his maps, dispatched a courier to General Lewenhaupt in Riga ordering him to follow the King with his 11,000 men, and turned abruptly southward into Ukraine.

Historians have pondered the causes of Charles' choice of invasion route, his decision to step off the main line from Smolensk to Moscow, which was the Napoleonic route a century later, for an expedition into Ukraine. It was not simply another unreasoned whim of the Swedish monarch but indicated more careful thought about the practical elements of the campaign than he had given the whole concept of a Muscovite invasion a year earlier. But, then, Charles XII was all his life a man of war; his inability to think like a statesman did not necessarily preclude him from thinking like a soldier.

First there was the question of fortifications. Peter had strongly barricaded the Smolensk-Moscow route and Charles knew that a direct march would be a tough siege campaign. Ukraine, however, offered a northward pass above the town of Poltava long used by Tatar raiders to penetrate into the heart of Muscovy. Charles might seize an open road to Moscow which bypassed Peter's fortifications. There was also, of course, the question of winter quarters and supplies; ravaged Livonia could not bear his army, but the crop-heavy barns of black soil Ukraine, basking in a comparatively milder climate and as yet untouched by war, beckoned invitingly.

Charles also believed that there were allies in Ukraine. The Crim Tatars and their Turkish overlords would lend their aid and Poltava would open the routes to them. Most attractive of all, Charles had reason to believe that the Cossacks of the Ukraine would join his cause. Charles was not the first invader or the last to base his expectations of success on a popular insurrection of the inhabitants against their rulers. Ivan Mazepa, Hetman of Ukraine, had been in contact with Charles for more than a year.

Ivan Mazepa, born around 1642, had been raised in Poland, educated by the Jesuits, had traveled in western Europe, and had been elected Hetman of Ukraine with the assistance of Vasili Golitsin, who sought maximum Cossack aid in his Crimean campaigns. The tasks of the Hetman were complex and demanding, since he had constantly to reconcile Muscovite overlordship with the traditional Cossack freedoms. Peter's demands after Narva had struck hard at those freedoms, laying heavy taxes, conscriptions, and discipline upon the Cossacks. Alexander Menshikov, the Tsar's agent in Ukraine, threatened Mazepa's authority. The Hetman, seeking to protect his leadership of the ruling oligarchy and to protect the autonomy of his land, began to discuss an alliance with Charles in the spring of 1708. In October of that year, Mazepa switched his allegiance; far better for Ukraine and for Mazepa, he thought, to ally with a foreign ruler located across the distant Baltic who would touch Ukraine but little, than to suffer the complete immersion in Muscovy which Peter's war policies seemed to demand. The Mazepa affair was another sign of the strains caused by Peter's early reforms and of the stresses inherent in a nascent Empire.

So, armed with substantial reasons for his Ukrainian detour, Charles led his army into the steppe. His target was Poltava and his prize was the northern pass to Moscow. Actually, long before he saw the walls of that obscure provincial town, the power of Charles had begun to erode. Menshikov had cut off Lewenhaupt in October at the battle of Lesnaya, "the mother of Poltava," inflicting severe losses on the Swedish reinforcements and seizing all their artillery and supplies. Within a few weeks the failure of the Swedes to retake the mouth of the Neva River with a land campaign from Finland insured Peter against a second front. The Tsar, acting with an assurance which must have impressed even Charles with the differences that seven years could make, swiftly seized and fortified the routes northward from Poltava, and Charles prepared to spend his winter in Ukraine in expectation of a spring campaign.

Even worse news awaited the Swedish King in Ukraine. The Turks and their Tatar satellites did not move to his aid; Peter had spent all of 1708 building a fleet at Voronezh and staging maneuvers at sea in order to warn off the Sultan, and his threats were successful. More startling still was the failure of Mazepa; the Hetman delivered only 2000 Cossacks to Charles. Peter, often warned about Mazepa, was still shocked: "for twenty-one years he has been faithful to me and now on the brink of the grave he has turned traitor to me and to his people." The Orthodox Church excommunicated Mazepa for dealing with the Protestants, Menshikov seized and burned his headquarters at Baturin, and a new Hetman, Ivan Skoropadsky, was elected with the Tsar present at the ceremony. "The people of Little Russia," wrote Peter, "stand more firmly than was possible to expect." Charles ignored all advice from his generals to retreat from this drastically altered situation or at least to await the arrival of substantial reinforcements before risking an engagement. In June, 1709, with the first decent traces of spring, Charles XII laid siege to the town of Poltava.

The Swedish army which surrounded Poltava on the right bank of the river Vorskla numbered 22,000 men and 30 guns. Peter came up on the opposite bank, calling in his far-flung troops until they numbered better than 40,000 men and 75 guns. The Tsar soon learned that the garrison in the town could not long withstand the siege and moved his troops northward along the river in search of a crossing. On June 19, as he effected that crossing, he issued his general orders to the Muscovite army:

> The hour has struck when the fate of the whole fatherland lies in your hands; either Russia will perish or she will be reborn in nobler form. And the army must not think of itself as armed and formed to fight for Peter, but for the Russian Tsardom entrusted to Peter by his birth and by the all-Russian people.

The details of the Battle of Poltava are blurred in every respect; not even the participants were sure of what happened on its bloody field. By June 24 Peter had moved his hasty works to within a mile of the besieging Swedes, and the peculiarities of terrain had left those works facing west rather than south. The Muscovites were formed in a quadrilateral, with woods on the north and south, so that their backs were to the river and only the west was open to a plain. Peter had built six redoubts across this opening, and four at right angles so that two narrow alleys led from the plain to the main Russian force. Charles did not hesitate before these formidable fortifications; already wounded in the foot on the nineteenth, he was carried about on pikes as he detached 13,000 men from the siege to meet his old enemy.

At dawn of June 27, Charles XII launched four infantry and six cavalry columns against Peter's works, and the nature of those works divided the field into two different battles. The action raged between early morning and noon, with both monarchs seemingly everywhere among their troops. The Tsar had several horses shot from under him. At one point in the confusion a Swedish regiment captured one of Peter's redoubts and the shout went up of Swedish victory. But this was not Narva, and the loss of a gun battery was no signal for chaos. Muscovite discipline was unshakeable and their counterattacks and withering crossfire levelled rank after rank of the Swedes. Charles lost 3,000 dead and 2,000 prisoners, while Peter lost only 1,300 men. So heady

was the victory, so magnificent the sense of relief, and so exuberant
the celebrations in the raucous Petrine manner, that the Tsar forgot
about the enemy; only at about five in the evening did Peter rouse himself to send his troops in chase. The remnants of the Swedish army
now scuttling for Moldavia were rounded up to the tune of 12,000 men.
King Charles himself fled the field, some say disguised as a peasant
woman, and made for Turkey.

Peter's reactions to his victory radiated joy and a growing sense of
its meaning. To his new mistress, Catherine, he wrote in plain happi-
ness: "Hello, little mother, I declare to you that the all-merciful God
has this day granted us an unprecedented victory over our enemies.
In a word, the whole of the enemy's army is knocked upon the head
and you will hear about it all soon from us." Peter wrote to Apraxin
with the sense that the Baltic coast had been won in the plains of
Ukraine: "Now with the help of God the final stone in the foundation
of Petersburg has been laid." Henceforth Peter spoke of Poltava as
"our resurrection."

Poltava was indeed important, although few contemporaries appreciated that importance clearly. It marked the end of a century of
Swedish power and it certainly reconstituted the shattered alliance
against the Swedes. At the same time, as Peter had seen immediately,
the battle guaranteed the Baltic coast to the Muscovites and even
foretold their expansion into Estonia and Livonia in the wake of their
weakened Polish ally. Poltava also assured Peter's role in the restoration of Augustus in Poland and thus signified his new dominance in
the affairs of that Republic. Russia had become a great European
power. The battle had domestic implications as well: the Cossack
communities had lost their autonomy in the midst of this struggle of
kings. Even more, Peter had confirmed for himself the value of the
reforms he had so urgently undertaken.

Given the extent of the Russian victory, the historian is hard-pressed
to explain why it took so long to put the seal of peace upon it. The
victory of Poltava came in 1709, but the peace treaty which organized
its results was not signed until 1721. Twelve years of anticlimax need
explanation, and that explanation rests partly in Peter's abounding
overconfidence and desire to expand the significance of his victory as
widely as possible. That egotism and diffusion of effort was demonstrated in his campaign against the Turk in 1711, in his pursuit of
dynastic marriages along the Baltic coast, in the growing resentment
of foreign enemies and allies alike of Peter's new and menacing role,

and in Peter's own roving mind which was willingly distracted by a thousand trifles when the war should have been prosecuted straight to its conclusion.

Peter's campaign on the Pruth was sufficient in itself to explain the failure to capitalize on Poltava. Relations between Muscovy and the Turks obviously deteriorated after Poltava, if only because the Turkish hope that the Swedes would level their enemy had been disappointed. Charles XII and his party were working with the aid of loans from the English Levant Company to awaken the Turk to the Muscovite menace. The Turks had reason enough since the fall of Azov to appreciate these warnings. The Sultan told Peter's ambassador that he would "sooner open his harem to the Russians as the Black Sea."

Peter, rather than negotiate or await a Turkish campaign which would draw the enemy far from home, happily took up this challenge as an opportunity to complete the military work he had begun. Peter would strike deep into Turkish territory before they could attack him, and the Turk would follow the Swede to defeat. Thus, Poltava, as did Narva with Charles XII, inflated Peter's ambitions. The conclusion of the Swedish war took second place to this new and glorious challenge.

The Tsar mapped out a grand strategy against the Turks with troops converging on the Pruth from Poland and from the Ukraine. He would respond to the call of Orthodox leaders in Moldavia and Wallachia who promised an uprising. Wrote the Hospodar [Christian Governor] of Wallachia: "We all pray with tears for the Sovereign Monarch to save us from the *piasts* [Polish nobles] and the Jesuits, who rage against the Orthodox more than against the Turk and Jew." For the first time, the Russian Tsar presented himself as the champion of Balkan Christians. Peter even issued a call for a Serbian revolt, and Saava Grutza of Dalmatia, a Petrine advisor for ten years, could be well pleased that his patron had finally taken up his cause. When Muscovite troops crossed the Dniester into Moldavia in May of 1711, the Hospodar Kantemir, father of one of the great Russian poets of the coming age, Prince Antioch Kantemir, declared his allegiance to the Tsar.

Peter and his mistress Catherine joined the army for the long march southward into the heart of Turkish territory, crossing the Pruth in late June, and in July came into contact with the Turkish army which had been massing against the Muscovites. The Turkish Grand Vizier and the Khan of Crimea had gathered about 190,000 men against Peter's 40,000. Ignorance was the order of the day; an English soldier with Peter said that "it was very surprising that we had not the least intelligence of so numerous an army which consisted of no less than 200,000 men until they were within sight of us." It was just as well for Peter's peace of mind that he was badly informed about the numbers ranged against him, and just as well for his survival that the Turkish intelligence was equally poor. The Orthodox Christians did not rise and the victor of Poltava found himself deep in unknown territory surrounded by an immense army whose outlines he could only dimly detect. A three-day battle at Stanzlishte cost him serious casualties. Disaster seemed imminent.

Peter was fortunate; fortunate that the Turks did not fully appreciate his plight and fortunate that they too were in difficulties. The Janissaries were recalcitrant and worried about politics at home, and the Turkish leaders greatly resented the influence of Charles XII, who had been forbidden to accompany the army. Peter knew that he had come too far and asked for talks. He told his agents that he was willing to pay any cost to extricate himself: he would surrender Azov, relinquish all Swedish conquests except Ingria, recognize Stanislaus Lesczynski as King of Poland, pay a tribute to the Sultan, even hand over the army if he would be allowed to depart. "Concede everything they want except slavery."

Happily, the Grand Vizier never made such demands and Peter's negotiators did not have to carry out their emergency instructions. Azov was to be returned to the Turks and other Muscovite fortifications dismantled. Peter promised to withdraw from Cossack and Polish affairs (a promise he did not intend to keep), retract his representation from the Porte, and permit Charles XII free passage to Sweden. On July 12, Peter signed and thanked God that he had escaped so easily. Europe never really knew how close the new soldier-hero had come to total reversal. The Tsar dragged his feet on all terms and the Turkish frontier was not really quiet again until the formal Treaty of Adrianople in 1713. No wonder, then, that the Swedes did not surrender.

Equally representative of Peter's squandering of his Poltava victory was the series of dynastic arrangements which he inflicted on his family and his posterity. He could not resist the temptation to play a great role and to remind his fellow monarchs how far he had come since 1697. He visited Germany in 1712, Finland in 1713, and Paris in 1717. A list of the marriages he arranged after Poltava will demonstrate his propensity for dynastic ties: Alexei, his son, to Charlotte von Wolfenbuettel, sister-in-law of the Austrian Emperor, in 1711; Anne, his step-niece (daughter of co-Tsar Ivan V) to the Duke of Courland, in 1710; Catherine, sister of Anne, to the Duke of Mecklenberg, in 1716; Anne, daughter by Catherine I, to the Duke of Holstein-Gottorp, in 1724; proposed marriage of Elizabeth, daughter by Catherine I, to Louis XV, in 1717, never arranged. (See chart on p. 166.)

While it is easy to appreciate Peter's temptation to marry his relatives into the ancient houses of Europe as a mark of his triumph and new acceptability, and while it is important to note that he was no busier at this game than his fellow monarchs, it would be well to consider the implications of these marriages more closely. Peter elevated himself into the company of such dynasts as Augustus of Saxony, Elizabeth Farnese, and the House of Hapsburg, but he did so by making himself the ally of some of the most repugnant rulers in Europe. He confused the internal politics of Russia for generations by injecting foreign houses and their interests; for the unhappy history of the monarchy in the eighteenth century is outlined in the above list. And, of course, he helped to prolong the war by convincing many European statesmen that Russia intended to penetrate Germany and make the Baltic a Muscovite lake; the marriage of Russians into Courland, Mecklenburg, and Holstein could only seem some sweeping strategy to encompass northern Europe.

Peter's pursuit of dynastic schemes, his victory over Sweden, his obvious role in the restoration of Augustus in Poland, and his new Baltic presence, all helped to arouse European resentment of Muscovy's new power. That growing fear in enemy and ally alike was the most substantial reason for Peter's failure to secure a rapid peace with the Swede; too many states had too much to fear from Muscovy's expansion. With the end of Louis XIV's war in 1713, Europe was able to pay more attention to the "Muscovite menace." Britain, with a Hanoverian on her throne so sensitive to German interests, was fearful for the Baltic and for Germany; Prussia worried about encirclement by Muscovite marriages; Austria resented Muscovite pretensions in the Balkans; France feared for its clients in Sweden and Poland. Everyone threw diplomatic obstacles in the way of Peter's conclusion of the war: "My allies are too many gods for me; what I want, they do not permit; what they advise, I cannot put into practice." Between 1712 and 1717, Peter had reason enough to feel that his resurrected coalition was more apparent than real; each of his allies had substantial reason to resist further Russian gains. Even the entry of Hanover and Prussia into the war against Sweden in 1715 was not intended as aid to Peter but only a means to insure their share of the spoils and to limit Muscovite control of the war. Peter planned an invasion of Sweden in 1716 to be assisted by the Danish navy, but the Danes procrastinated and ultimately prevented the invasion from ever coming to pass. The naive Tsar was slowly being taught the lessons of European politics.

One can sympathize a bit with Peter if by 1717 he began to lend an ear to schemes of great imagination but doubtful worth to bring the war to a conclusion. Peter was searching for some way out from between the obstinance of his enemies and the perversity of his allies. A visit to Paris in 1717 to convince the French to throw over their Swedish ties and to accept Muscovy as their new counterweight in the north was just such a move. Peter was entertained by the Regent and lionized by society but the treaty of friendship which was signed meant nothing to the French. In 1717 also, Peter listened to a Holstein adviser of Charles XII, Baron Goertz, who recommended a Swedish-Russian alliance to dominate northern Europe, with Muscovy keeping all its conquests and compensating Sweden with provinces torn from Hanover, Denmark, and Prussia. The Goertz scheme was written on the wind, but Peter was in a mood for such facile solutions.

The whole picture was severely altered in December, 1718, when Charles XII was killed in a local battle in Norway. He was succeeded by his sister Ulrica Eleanora whose policy, guided by her husband, Frederick of Hesse-Cassel, reverted to traditional lines. Goertz and his Holstein clique were executed, and Sweden hastened to come to terms with all belligerents except Muscovy. It was a good time, for the death of Charles, added to Muscovite victories, convinced most states that the disintegration of Sweden was near at hand. Everyone except Peter came to make peace in 1718–19: Hanover got Bremen and Verden, Prussia got Stettin, and Augustus got his Polish throne. Peter, wondering what effect this mass defection of allies would have, proceeded to an invasion and conquest of Finland which confirmed his view that Muscovy was far better off without its friends.

The defection of Muscovy's allies was accompanied by a growing Anglo-Swedish friendship, and in 1720 England promised naval assistance. George of Hanover, ever minding his German store, was busy using English diplomatic machinery to create a league between Britain, Hanover, the Empire, Saxony, and Poland against Russia and Prussia. Russia and England were drawing close to open war, but the

South Sea Bubble drew in English horns, discouraged the Swedes, and inspired a series of Russian strikes against the Swedish coast. Sweden, exhausted and friendless, sued for peace.

The meetings at Nystadt in Finland finally produced a treaty in August, 1721. Peter got Livonia, Ingria, Estonia, part of Karelia with Vibourg, and the islands in the gulf of Finland, "for all time to come." For his part, the Tsar agreed to return Finland, to pay 2 million Dutch thalers, to renounce interference in Swedish affairs, and to protect the rights of the inhabitants in the ceded territories. The Muscovites kept their terms; the Baltic barons were indeed protected in their control of the local populations, governing themselves under their own laws and coming in droves into Peter's service. During the massive celebrations of 1721, the All-Governing Senate voted Peter a new title as "Most August Emperor of All the Russias" and the imperial era of Russian history was born. Peter commissioned a fountain for his summer palace at Peterhof in which a jet of water eighty feet high shoots from the jaws of the Nemean lion being ripped open by a gilded Hercules; thus did the new Hercules rip the Baltic from the Swede.

The account of Peter's wars usually ends with the Peace of Nystadt, a fitting historical climax to the main business of the age. Unfortunately, Peter did not think to please historians nor did he really consider that his reign was over in 1721, to be followed by four years of anticlimax. In 1722, although western Europeans hardly noticed and historians include it as an afterthought, Peter took 100,000 men into Persia on a hard campaign to insure Russian interests in the Persian trade, to secure the shores of the Caspian, and to extend his protection to the Shah. All of these things he accomplished by the Treaty of Saint Petersburg in 1723. Peter was a ruler with vital interests around the periphery of his vast holdings and not simply a supplicant barbarian at the altar of "westernization." It would be foolish to downgrade the vital role and significance of the Great Northern War to Muscovy, but it would be equally as foolish to fall into some "western" myopia and to ignore the wider interests of the Tsar: Peter looked south and east as well as west, and was laying the foundations of a continental empire as vast and as promising as the overseas settlements of his western European counterparts. If Russia was declared an Empire in 1721, the strip of Baltic coastline was but a part of it.

Peter's war achieved its goal and more, and in this the Tsar was, if anything, more successful than his fellow European monarchs. It may help to set Peter in a better image than that of the proverbial "student" to recall that Peter's war was far more successful and more profitable to his empire than the debilitating wars of Louis XIV, or those of Sweden, Austria, or Spain in this age. This most satisfactory soldier in a generation of soldiers brought within the confines of his empire the Baltic coast, with its prosperous cities of Riga, Dorpat, and Revel. He was a maker of kings in Poland where Augustus was restored and in Persia where the Shah accepted his protection. He had permanently interested his state in the business of western Europe and sat astride the Baltic, many of whose petty princes were incorporated into his family. He had invoked Orthodox brotherhood for the first time beyond the ancient boundaries of Muscovy. He had secured the frontiers of his realm as his father and grandfather had dreamed of doing. And, most universal of all effects, he had reorganized his realm from top to bottom for the accomplishment of all these tasks. Thus, as with the other successful monarchs of his day, the organization for conquest lasted longer and with more significance than the conquest itself. Men, resources, church, industry, commerce, all required an immense relocation for the heavy tasks of war. And there is the connection between war and reform, a connection as important in other parts of Europe as it was in Petrine Russia.

The most obvious products of the Petrine wars were the army and navy. An army of 130,000 men, with another 100,000 Cossack auxiliaries and troops of subject nationalities had been created, easily the largest in Europe. A sophisticated and articulated military administration produced a general staff, two field marshals, and thirty field generals (of whom fourteen were foreigners), a Military College, a Naval College, a Supply Commissariat, and a Recruit Supply Office. By 1725 the number of foreigners in Peter's army was no larger and often far smaller than in most European armies of the day; thirty years later the French army would still have over 50,000 foreign mercenaries, and the Prussians, Spanish, and Austrians had large foreign contingents. Further, Russia was almost alone in Europe in recruiting most of its army forcibly from the general population, certainly a most "modern" practice which western European governments would ultimately emulate.

By 1725 the navy had come even further. The army reforms had been the refinement and enlargement of the work of Tsar Alexei and Vasili Golitsin, but the navy grew from almost nothing. Its growth was more amazing since the original naval work of Peter before 1700, the Azov fleet, was scuttled after the Pruth campaign. By 1725 there were 48 ships of the line, 750 auxiliary vessels, and 28,000 sailors, all on the Baltic. Shipyards were busy at Petersburg, Kronstadt, and Olonetz. There were relatively far more foreigners in high commands in the navy than in the army, which was only natural in an establishment of such recent vintage. The startling aspect of this naval growth and its obvious role in exciting new fears in Europe can be appreciated if one recalls that in 1710 there had not been one Russian battleship in the Baltic, while fifteen years later the Muscovite fleet was larger than that of the Danes and Swedes combined.

But military numbers and organization only begin to tell the impact of the war. The Russian army reforms of the seventeenth century which culminated in Peter's work eliminated dependence on a feudalized nobility or a privileged *streltsi* and established a centrally sustained army under the ruler's command. Nothing was more important to the development of Russian absolutism than this response to the demanding military tasks of the seventeenth and early eighteenth centuries. As a consequence, the ruler inevitably assumed the weight of military expenses; as has been seen, 63 per cent of the state budget in 1725 was military, and in that year there was no war! The responsibilities for waging war were lifted by the ruler out of the hands of the nobility and bodyguards and reimposed upon the whole population, which previously had been free of such service. This shift in military and financial responsibility exalted the absolute state and required centralization, enumeration, discipline, articulation, and the imposition of duties upon all subjects of the crown. Surely the population in service as against the nobility in service is a "modern" concept; yet Peter did not so much learn this concept from "the west" as to assist other European monarchs yet to come to see the practical uses of the concept more clearly. Peter was a "military modernizer" as much as a "student of the west"; he was himself an important formulator of some aspects of what we call the modern world.

And so the Great Northern War was more than a war for the lost Baltic coast or for "windows to the west," although Peter's aspirations for empire were as real and as pressing as Louis XIV's drive for the natural boundaries of France or Frederick William's search after geographical and administrative unity for his Electorate. It was also a war for control of the kingdom, in which the varied forces of resistance to the monarch's will were given the deathblow after a century and more of struggle. Voltaire was right when he said that

Russia was wagering much in the Great Northern War; a loss might well have meant a return to the weaknesses of the Time of Troubles, as a substantial loss for Louis XIV might have meant a return to the weaknesses of France's sixteenth century. Great wars, then, demanded great reorganizations, and, unpleasant thought though it may be to many modern minds, those kingdoms in the seventeenth and eighteenth centuries which made the greatest wars for the longest time with some degree of success laid many of the foundations of the modern world.

※ 4 ※

Administration and Finance

Nothing is better designed to hasten even the most patient reader along in search of more dramatic chapters than a discussion of administration and finance. Yet anyone who has involved himself ever so slightly in administrative affairs on any level learns lessons about the centers of power and the importance of budgetary controls, and may even be rewarded with substantial insights into the human ambitions and broader policies which these financial accounts and administrative blueprints often conceal. The administrative and financial policies of Peter the Great are revealing; they expose the search for a viable central government apparatus, the attempt to supply the ever-mounting needs of war and great power, and the emerging requirement of an extensive supply of trained manpower to give flesh to the structure.

Russia was not peculiar in its attempts to reshape administration in more modern design, for this was the European age of administrative reform. Politically, governments were convinced that the power of the monarch was only as effective as the bureaucracy which implemented it. Philosophically, governments were certain with Montesquieu that regulated and well-defined administrative apparatus was a firm guarantee of efficient government and of social order. Practically, governments were tinkering with their machinery in search of expanded sources of revenue. Monarchs were building more organized bureaucracies to extract larger revenues from more subjects in order to put their realm in order and to fight larger and more demanding wars. At the same time there was an astonishing assurance among European statesmen that the reorganization of offices and the redrawing of lines of command would in turn alter the nature of their whole system; this assurance is common among politicians and businessmen of every age, but it was particularly prevalent among Peter and his fellow monarchs. Some historians would lay this condition to the popularization of Newton's mechanical universe, indicating that observation of the universe of natural regulations impelled statesmen to seek harmony with nature by searching out the natural regulations and proper order of their governments. Others might say that administrative tinkering is always preferred by rulers to true social or economic reform, for administrative alterations are at least within their power to accomplish. Still others, including the author, might absolve poor Newton so early in the century and simply say that monarchs, sharing and responding to the fears of political chaos which had besieged most European states in the seventeenth century, and faced with ever-increasing internal and external tasks, had of necessity to involve themselves in the elaboration of government machinery or surrender their concepts of absolutism. That they had such faith in their administrative tinkering only testifies that they lived and innovated so early in the modern era that they escaped its endemic disease of cynicism.

But while it was surely true that government administrations in many parts of Europe were being overhauled to strengthen the hold of the monarch on his subjects and to improve the collection of funds and the efficiency of their use, administration in some parts of eastern Europe, especially in Prussia and in Russia, had an importance all its own. As Professor M. S. Anderson has pointed out, the administrative structure here was really the only "constitution" of the state;[1] there were no intermediate bodies with rights distinct from the crown sheltered behind an autonomous judicial structure of some form, for in Muscovy the courts were but another arm of the monarch's will. This condition explains why even the Church would be included within the administrative framework before the reign of Peter was done. Thus, "constitutionalism," meant only an efficient, well-ordered and internally consistent administrative system to implement the autocratic will of the ruler. For Prussia such a regulated and unified administration was the response to the geographical disunity of the realm, while for Russia it was the response to its geographical vastness. In the absence of intermediate bodies and local initiatives present in

---

[1] M. S. Anderson, *Europe in the Eighteenth Century 1713–1783* (New York: Holt, Rinehart & Winston, Inc., 1961), p. 89.

some European systems, the success of the autocratic form in governing the realm was quite accurately seen to be bound up totally with the order and efficiency of its administration. In such circumstances the administrative structure was of more than peripheral interest.

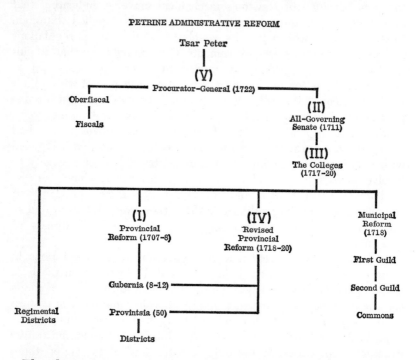

PETRINE ADMINISTRATIVE REFORM

The chart of Petrine administration as of Peter's death is doubly deceptive. Every chart is by nature a reassuring device, for its sharp lines, its air of order, its crisp delineation of chains of command devoid of human idiosyncrasy, all serve to reassure the viewer that all is well and that even he, outsider though he be, can easily perceive the heart of the matter; this may explain the popularity of charts with politicians, university presidents, and corporate executives. But any chart of Peter's administration is deceptive, first because it communicates a sense of planning and order in its creation which was never present, and second because it serves to convey the idea that it worked as well as it looked. As antidote for the first deception, note that the administrative chart also marks the chronology of the major elements of the reform and that the chronology belies a master plan.

For the second deception the only antidote is discussion of the administration itself.

The first provincial reform of the years 1707–08 was clearly defined by the period in which it was made, and perhaps "reform" is too gracious a word for the clumsy expedients of those years. The era between the defeat at Narva and the victory at Poltava was dominated by policies of state salvation. The danger of disaster was clear, the overwhelming importance of military organization was obvious, and the concern of the Tsar for a coming invasion of his lands was obsessive. Consequently the "reform" of 1707–08 was haphazard in its creation and was directed exclusively to problems of defense preparedness. Here were no grand visions of a Russian future but instinctive responses to the pressures of a war to be won or a throne to be lost.

Peter in the years after the defeat at Narva governed his realm from his pocket. The Tsar had never been willing to settle into the sedentary style of Muscovite government since his accession, and the rigors of military preparation for Azov, the journeys through Europe, and the general reorganization after Narva did not encourage him to do so. His capacity for work on the move was enormous and his aides were ground into exhaustion by his itinerary alone. Beginning in 1700 and continuing through 1708, those close to Peter were randomly assigned to go into various parts of the state and organize them for the war effort by extracting from them the maximum in men, money, and supplies: Tikhon Streshnev to Moscow, Michael Golitsin to Ukraine, Alexander Menshikov to Ingria, P. M. Apraxin to Kazan, Matthew Gagarin to Siberia, Peter Golitsin to Archangel, F. M. Apraxin to Azov, and Peter Saltykov to Smolensk. The first provincial "reform" merely formalized this personal device of the Tsar for extorting and expediting military requirements and its central point was to put the maintenance of the Muscovite army on a territorial basis, an admission that the lands were too vast and the central machinery too limited to do anything but decentralize military business. For this purpose agents would reside in the countryside, since Peter believed that far more could be extracted from the peasants by officials on the scene and much more in resources would ultimately arrive at the army if the old corrupt channels were avoided. The Muscovite realm was divided into eight large *gubernia,* based on the former military districts of the Tsar Fyodor and on the ad hoc assignments of Peter's fledglings. The territorial organization of many of the old Muscovite *prikazi* made this decentralization rather easy.

The governor, a little tsar in his own *gubernia*, as Professor John Wolf called the intendant of France "a little king in his généralité," [2] had four assistants for tax collection, grain collection, troop collection, and prosecution of shirkers. Orders, money, conscripts, and food supplies now bypassed the central administration, and in 1711 the regiments of the army were directly attached to the *gubernia* through commissars.

The purposes of this provincial "reform" seem obvious even from the obligations of the provincial officers which it created: to increase the flow of resources directly to designated regiments at the front. No one would reasonably criticize Peter's logic as he faced the threat of a Swedish invasion, but neither would anyone wish to conceive of this system as a visionary reform for the future government of Russia. The governors, when they did visit their supposedly permanent posts, acted like foreign conquerors; a report from Kazan province represented many others when it complained that it was "impossible to collect not only the extraordinary but even the ordinary levies because of the great increase in the number of abandoned households." The problem inherent in an administrative system which ignored any central accounting and which defined "to govern" as "to extract" were substantial.

The first provincial reorganization assisted the rapid disappearance of the central government of Muscovy. The *prikazi* in Moscow were now replaced by provincial offices doing their primary business directly with the army; many *prikazi* dried up and blew away in neglect, while others resolved themselves into provincial offices for Moscow province. At the same time this "reform" severely limited the scope of government, for it valued only the arts of extortion; agencies with more creative duties were allowed to atrophy. The role of the Tsar did nothing to stop this drift to decentralization and abnegation of responsibility but rather accentuated it. Peter was the peripatetic Tsar, first in the north surveying the construction of Petersburg, then in the south at Azov, then in the west along the fortified frontier. Chaos and despair pervaded the remaining central offices of state while the Tsar's pockets bulged with the business of government wherever he was; those closest to him in geography and in spirit became the experts of the moment in the solution of pressing problems, and the building of

[2] John Wolf, *The Emergence of the Great Powers 1685–1715* (New York, 1951), p. 99.

Romanov absolutism seemed to have regressed to its clumsiest beginnings as a "system of delegation." The lack of coordination of information and resources created by an eight-headed administration with no central headquarters, together with the vastly improved opportunities for corruption, would ultimately have appalled even an administration-hater like Tsar Peter. After Poltava, when the decentralization had done its work as a tool of war and had begun to reveal its overwhelming inadequacy as a tool of government, there was time to consider its future with more vision. It would be fairer to say that what is usually called the "provincial reform" of 1707–08 was rather a series of wartime expedients whose chaotic consequences precipitated honest reform. These expedients had a certain relationship to the view of the philosopher Leibniz so often conveyed to Peter, that the more blank the tablet upon which reform was to be written the less resistance would the reform encounter; the provincial expedients helped to erase a good deal of the administrative structure of old Muscovy and to invite new undertakings.

A major element in the Petrine administration emerged in the wake of Poltava—the All-Governing Senate. Peter's reforms had created eight local units but had thereby cut the roots of central government, and Russia could not manage long without restoration of some institutional center. Truly, the effective authority of the Tsar could not be expected to survive Peter's reign in the prevailing circumstances. It used to be said that the Boyar Duma, the body of the Tsar's advisers, was replaced in 1711 by the establishment of the Senate. We know now that by 1711 the Boyar Duma had long ceased to operate, sent to death by neglect rooted in Peter's style of itinerant government and in the provincial reorganization. The Senate, the first step toward the reestablishment of central institutions, was created in haste to fill the vacuum. Peter, leaving for the campaign on the Pruth in 1711, was finally convinced that the government ought not to travel so far with him but ought instead to have a base from which his orders could be efficiently implemented. Even though it was presumed in 1711 that Peter's return to his capital would end the Senate's role as his substitute, his sterling record of non-attendance at his government posts effectively guaranteed its permanence. The Tsar's decree said that "we have appointed a Governing Senate to whose edicts all will be obedient as if it were we ourselves, under threat of severe punishment and death." The vote of the Senate was to be unanimous. The first nine Senators appointed in 1711 were not really "fledglings" of Peter and continued to be pressured by the whims of the Petrine favorites.

But the Senate was badly needed and its duties rapidly collected around it in testimony to that fact. It was never an advisory group such as the Boyar Duma, and became the chief administrative organ of the Tsar, not by any plan but because the Tsar ruled in the manner he did. Peter often sent brief notes to his Senate, as he did to all those under his orders, but such notes required interpretation, elaboration, and implementation to make them effective. For Peter to order that 5,000 men be sent to dredge his new naval base on the Sea of Azov was one thing, but finding the men, organizing their supplies, and arranging their transport were the tasks which the Senate was obliged to interpolate and fulfill. There is even some thought that in reality the Senate thus exercised legislative power in transforming the staccato messages of their Tsar into full-blown orders for all Muscovy. The Senate also rapidly acquired the role of a central judicial body, a court of appeals, once again because the Tsar was too busy to sit in person and exercise his prerogatives. No historian has ever successfully tied the creation of this multifaceted Senate to any foreign models.

The primary work of the Senate, because it was the primary work of the Tsar, was the organization of men and money for war. Peter's original decree charged the Senators to "collect as much money as possible!" The provincial decentralization could not serve such campaigns as the distant march on the Pruth efficiently, and the Senate was now charged with this responsibility. The slowness and independence of his provincial governors had frustrated and even frightened the Tsar; in a letter to Menshikov in early 1711 he complained that "up to now God knows my grief, for my governors are like crabs in performing their duties . . . and consequently I shall henceforth deal with them with my hands rather than with words." The Tsar was ignorant even of Menshikov's activities in his province, "thus I know no more about your province than I would about some foreign country." Slowly the machinery of central government recovered itself as the Senate was connected to the provinces. Provincial officials were obliged to submit their reports and to turn over their tax collections directly to the Senate, and commissars charged with the task of tying capital and provinces together were under threat of severe penalties to perform their tasks conscientiously. Further elaboration of the work of the Senate was provided by the *Oberfiscal* and the *fiscals*, agents

appointed by the Senate to search out corruption and maladministra-
tion in the supply lines. *Fiscals* were commissioned to bring their
charges directly to the Senate, and these "eyes and ears of the Senate"
were soon spread up and down the administration. Institutions at last
began again to transform the personal dynamism of Peter into the
permanent authority of the Tsardom.

The obvious need for such permanent institutions as the Senate may
serve to obscure its difficulties. The authority of the Senators was
never clearly established and the temporary nature of the Senate's
creation was never regularized although it lasted as an institution
until the end of the monarchy. In Peter's day the provincial governors
ignored its decrees when they could and fought innumerable battles
with it about the extent of their authority, while the subsidiary departments of the central government were so demoralized that they
offered the Senate little help in its tasks. Emphasis on the abstract
lines of administration also obscures the fact that the administrators
themselves were suspect in character, deprived in education, and
limited in vision. Many of Peter's Senators had to be watched constantly by the Tsar, for they could not be trusted to share his en-
thusiasms, his abilities, or his honesty. Peter put an Inspector-General
over the Senate in 1715 and in 1722 created the office of Procurator-
General of the Senate for one of his favorites. This "sovereign's eye"
was to organize the tasks of the Senate, to act in the Tsar's place in
their discussions, to give the Tsar's approval to decrees, and to enforce
the Tsar's will on the Senate. He was to insure by some magical means
that "the Senators will work honestly, energetically, and efficiently."

The next major stage of administrative reform was a necessary
consequence of the restoration of central institutions, and at the same
time evidenced the growing sense of planning on the part of a more
experienced Tsar. The "college" system was the product of the increasing volume of work laid upon the Senate, and, some historians insist,
of the permanent residence provided for the Russian government for
the first time in a decade by the transfer of the Senate to the new
capital at Saint Petersburg. In order to expedite the work of the
central government, nine "colleges," similar in function to ministries,
were announced in 1717 and organized over the following three years.
This reform was given material embodiment in the new college buildings which the Tsar demanded of the architects of his flourishing
capital.

The collegial principle of organization was a common phenomenon in Europe in Peter's day, especially in Prussia, Sweden, and Austria. Peter's correspondent, the philosopher Leibniz, wrote to the Tsar that "there can be good administration only with colleges; their mechanism is similar to that of watches, whose wheels serve to keep one another in motion." There was something so appealing and reassuring in such images of machine-like order for states which, having emerged from political anarchy in all parts of Europe, feared chaos above all other evils. Actually, Peter had little choice in his models; his Muscovite heritage provided no clues except the clumsy *prikazi* and everywhere the government experts of Europe were trumpeting the praises of the collegial idea. It would have been astonishing if Peter had not adopted it for his own. Discussion of such a reform began in 1698, but only in 1712 did an experiment with a College of Commerce begin. Officials who had been sent by Peter to study the system in Sweden and advisers imported from Austria laid out the plans for its broader implementation. There was a new air of intent and planning about this phase of administrative reform which had so far been absent.

The nine colleges decreed in 1717 included foreign affairs, state income, financial control, justice, army, navy, commerce, mining and manufacture, and state expenses. Thus the haphazard work of the *prikazi* was to be reallocated along sensible lines. Each college, and this is the heart of the collegial principle, was composed of a board of eleven members which arrived at its decisions by majority vote. A college was staffed by a president, vice-president, four counsellors, four assessors, and a secretary. Thus Peter created a government by committee, since the college had no chief minister and was collectively responsible for its business. It was this form, as we shall soon see, which was so well adapted to striking down the central authority of the Patriarch and incorporating the Church into the administrative structure. Peter tended the national pride by installing Russians as presidents of all but one college, while appointing experienced foreigners as vice-presidents. It has been said that Peter adopted the college system because there were not enough responsible or honest leaders in Muscovy to whom state business could be individually entrusted, and that the colleges provided the means for mutual surveillance. This was essentially the argument of Charles XI of Sweden when he had implemented the same system a generation earlier, and Feofan Prokopovich, the Tsar's church adviser, wrote that "the truth is more surely discovered by joint endeavor than by a single person."

It would be fairer to say of Peter that he envisioned the college system as a school of state in which as many high administrators as possible could be involved in the learning process. Actually, many of the colleges rapidly devolved into one-man rule, especially where one of the favorites was involved.

Now, with some order and organization provided at the center, the final stage of the administrative reform became logically necessary. The provincial system of 1707–8 which glorified decentralization was by nature alien to the new central institutions; a foreign observer noted that "the chanceries in the provinces, from which business must come to the colleges in Saint Petersburg, still remained on the old footing and although instructions were sent to them how they must forward their reports and accounts, the old Russian clerks could not understand them and thus caused much disorder." And so the reform had come full cycle: a provincial decentralization had undermined central offices, new and hasty central institutions such as the Senate had required elaboration in the colleges, and the new central system had in turn required the refitting of the local government. The second provincial reform of 1718–20 tended to oversimplify the task and ended as the most unsatisfactory part of the reorganization, but that might be expected in this century and in this realm. Some historians have felt that the failure was largely explained by Peter's attempts to impose the local institutions evolved over centuries in tiny Sweden quickly upon the immense lands of Muscovy by sheer force. Perhaps the administration of an autocracy in such vast lands was bound to weaken in authority the farther one traveled from the throne no matter what the system, and local government was bound to be the weakest element in any system which had ceded its authority over the bulk of the peasant population into private hands.

The second provincial reform broadened, at least in theory, the purposes of local government beyond tax collection and conscription, and such change, even if but in theory, was an improvement. The large *gubernia* of 1708 were preserved for military purposes, while the primary units of the empire were now the *provintsia*, 50 in number. *Provintsia*, in turn broken down into districts, were administered by governors who were now salaried and who dealt directly with the central government. The salary was designed to end the idea of state officials living off the people, although few peasants would ever have noticed the change. The Swedish system was abandoned at this point and no attempt was made to impose Swedish forms of local government on the peasantry. The peasants, in other words, remained under the complete control of their landlords on the estates and there was still a great chasm between local government and the bulk of the Russian people. As in the Austrian system the will of the ruler was transferred to the nobility and, since serfdom was the basic fact of peasant life in Petrine Russia, one would hardly expect to see the creation of any peasant institutions outside the landlord's control. Nor did the new reform terminate the attachment of the army to geographical roots; the more than one hundred regimental districts were not abolished until 1727.

Because of the absence of basic local institutions in the new system, towns had to be provided for separately in the second provincial reform. The Baltic institutions of Riga served as models for what was in the main a sterile effort. It had been the plan of Ordyn-Nashchokin in the reign of Tsar Alexei to take towns out from under the stifling control of the military governors who fed on them, but *pomeshchik* pressure had cancelled his reform. Town population as listed in the first poll-tax census of 1718 showed about 170,000 males, of whom 40,000 qualified as merchants. This population was divided into two guilds based on wealth and status and a third and largest group of the "common people." All townsmen were subjected to the poll tax, but the two guilds were excused from military service. The business of the town was in the hands of a *magistrat*, formed of members of the first guild elected by the two guilds. The bulk of the population in the third category could neither vote nor hold office. The *magistrat* was charged with formidable tasks: taxation, security, justice, commercial expansion, industrial development, and the care of public welfare. But it spent most of its time protecting its own interests, avoiding government attention, and eluding government demands. Peter's decrees had little effect in generating that town prosperity which he had so much admired in the Baltic ports. Perhaps someone should have reminded him that in those Baltic towns it was prosperity which had bred the institutions and not the other way around. In 1727, with the Tsar buried and his expectations with him, towns were again subjected to the authority of local governors.

There were benefits produced by the new administrative system. By 1725 the Senate and the Colleges were beginning to divide their labors with the level of conflict now reduced from incredible to merely outrageous; for all the grinding and squealing of its parts, the machinery provided a far more rational division of work than did the old *prikazi.* The Colleges, administering their responsibilities on a national rather than a regional basis as had been the Muscovite habit, were on their way toward an "enlightened" goal of unified treatment of the entire empire. The most striking contribution was the change from a system designed in fact to reserve government to a tiny oligarchy to a system designed in theory to govern and protect the state. Offices now drew provincial nobles to the capital and laid upon them a sense of obligation to the state. It may have been only in theory that economic and social progress were posited as the aims of this new administration, but that thought was certainly better than the one which it replaced, and thought, perhaps, is father to the deed.

Finally, too much emphasis is constantly placed on the confusion in which Petrine administration was born and far too little on the fact that many of these institutions lasted for all of or a major part of the lifetime of the Russian Empire. Regardless of inferences about order and planning in other states, nowhere across Europe were administrations created according to any neat master plan. In most organizing states in Europe from the middle of the seventeenth century onward trial and error presided over the birth of government machinery. Far too much has been made, too, of the fact that war and military needs determined the shape of administrative growth in Russia. This was certainly true, but it was equally true for Prussia and France. There was nothing inherent in the war-centered birth of administrative structures which condemned them to inefficiency and sterility, for no one has anything but praise for Prussian accomplishments in this area.

At the same time the weaknesses of the administrative reforms were evident. The machinery was really a bequest to coming generations, for the friends of the Emperor were still as powerful at the end of the reign as they were in its early years. It was still essentially a government of persons rather than of institutions, a more sophisticated "system of delegation," in which proximity to the person of the Tsar was far more indicative of power than the holding of any office. The constant ignoring of and overriding of institutions was not only suffered by the Tsar but often abetted by him. Peter employed favorites or guardsmen for many tasks and thereby weakened both the structure and the morale of the civil service. The administration was never permitted to forget that the Tsar was an autocrat obliged to answer to no person, law, procedure, but who could override them and their regulations at his whim. Many of the weaknesses of the administrative structure survived as long as the structure itself, and this characteristic remained a permanent stumbling block to a "constitutional" administration for the duration of the monarchy.

Nor did the administrative changes really alter the nature of administrators, an additional reason for Peter to resort to his favorites. Inefficiency, stupidity, corruption, and often opposition to the Tsar's policies permeated the new administration as it had the old, but now the size and complexity of the system made it infinitely more difficult to root them out. Peter constantly threatened and carried out physical punishments against the highest officials who mishandled their trust, but the fact that such brutal handling increased in the last years of the reign is evidence that the medicine was ill-suited to the malady. The Tsar might will into existence an orderly government machine but he could not will into existence the men capable of using it. The work of reorganizing the government of Russia was the work of years, but the work of training the servants to staff it was the work of generations. Pososhkov, the merchant economist, was not speaking simply of popular resentment when he said that the Tsar pushed upward with the astonishing strength of ten men but was pressed down upon by the weight of thousands.

The primary task of administrations in this European age was the accumulation of revenues to carry on the work of the state. One of the reasons for the constant rearrangement of government offices was the notorious difficulty of tax gathering. Tax structures at the end of the seventeenth century were conspicuously "irrational," emerging haphazardly from the periods of chaos in the very recent past which were the heritage of almost every major European state. Yet with a tax structure limited by privileges and riddled with inequities, the wars in Europe still grew vastly more expensive than they had ever been as uniforms, arms, and supplies had now to be delivered over longer routes to larger contingents for longer periods of time. One of the satisfying substitutes for true tax reform was administrative reshuffling designed to better exploit the current resources of a realm.

Peter's approach to the financial conditions of his realm was strongly in the spirit of this age. He, as Colbert a generation before him, insisted to his Senate that "money is the arteries of war." Even the briefest comparison of the relation of military costs to total state revenues testifies in the strongest terms to the preeminent role of war in Petrine Russia. If money was indeed the arteries, or, depending upon your anatomical preferences, the sinews of war, then the collection of money was the government's primary concern. Peter's techniques for such collection varied from the crudest to the most sophisticated and from those of passing import to those with social impact for decades to come. Peter was the same man in finance as he was in war, a man of great capacity and strong will; action was his forte and results his sole concern.

Year	War Expenses (in million rubles)	Total Revenues (in million rubles)
1681	—	1.2
1701	2.270	3.0
1710	3.158	3.3
1725	5.5	8.5

The collection of money required first of all some sense of how much the government already took in revenue, from what sources, how it was dispersed, and whether it was sufficient. The government required the establishment of a state budget, a development which took place in Sweden only during the reign of Charles XI. The wars of the seventeenth century and the increasing imposition of taxes to fight them had prodded the Muscovite governments, as they had governments everywhere, toward such budgetary controls. Rudiments of such a budget emerged in the short reign of Fyodor, but it was for Peter to organize the practice. He established an Accounts Office to inquire into the financial conditions of all the *prikazi* and to present a general picture of the government's condition. The first balance sheet provided in 1710 indicated income of 3.3 million rubles and overall expenses of 3.8 million. Awareness of the true costs of programs and growing deficits drove Peter and his advisers to seek major alterations in the methods of state financing.

Peter debased the coinage of his realm with consistency and dedication, especially in the years between Narva and Poltava. The extent of the depreciation of the currency is not really known although most historians agree that the value of the ruble dropped substantially in Peter's reign. It is stylish to ridicule Peter's crude expedient, but the debasement of the coinage was only the most apparent manifestation of Peter's search for currency. The development of the economy and the demands of war investment required an immense expansion of money in circulation. Peter, harking back to the programs of the Commercial Code of 1667, had to forbid the exportation of precious metals and of Russian money, and had to attract precious metals into the country and reissue them as national currency. He had also to uncover mines for his own supplies of precious metals which were severely limited at his accession, and to debase the coinage already in circulation. Some of the copper church bells which escaped the confiscations for artillery after Narva ended up minted into coins. The results were not so ridiculous: Peter was able to issue in his reign over 30 million silver rubles through state mints and licensed smiths, and debasement had contributed about 3 million of them.

The tax practices of Petrine Russia followed and accelerated the movement of the seventeenth century. If we are to place any faith at all in the skimpy statistics available, indirect taxes had predominated in pre-Petrine Muscovy, comprising 47 per cent of state revenues as against 24 per cent for direct taxes in the 1670's. But even then more and more reliance was being placed on direct taxation, and more and more effort was bent to simplify and generalize that direct taxation over the realm. By the end of Peter's reign that drift to more simplified and more universal direct taxation had reached the point where 55 per cent of state revenues came from this source. The movement in this direction was cause for severe resentment in the population, and the cause also for unforeseen but potent consequences. Direct taxation laid the bulk of the burden of building the Petrine state on the backs of the Muscovite peasantry, for Peter in his reign floated not one foreign loan in the financial capitals of western Europe.

If the Petrine government was to utilize the traditional household tax which it inherited from the seventeenth century, then obviously the census would have to be revised to reflect contemporary conditions. The last census had been taken in 1678 and had been notoriously inaccurate; Muscovy suffered from the general European disease of tax bases which remained fabricated and fixed for generations. The Tsar insisted on a new accounting. The Petrine census of 1710 was a bitter shock to the Muscovite government, for it revealed a vast depopulation of the Russian countryside. The census of 1678 had arrived at a total of about 800,000 households subject to tax, while the census of 1710 could only accumulate less than 640,000.

Recovering from its initial disbelief, the Muscovite government began to evaluate its information. Slowly, the reasons for the "flight of people" emerged. It was clear first of all that the Muscovite definition of a "household" had been poor and that census takers had been badly instructed and supervised. It was clear also that the taking of statistics had been performed in a very clumsy manner by persons whose literacy was seriously in question, and here the effects of financial need in generating an educational system for bureaucrats is evident. More central and more revealing of the infinite resources of the Russian peasant for self-protection against the attacks of the state was the fact that while households had become fewer in number since 1678 they had also become larger in composition. Peasants had amalgamated households in order to avoid taxes, a practice which tended to decrease the amount of land in cultivation. Finally, of course, it was necessary to recognize that whatever other explanations could be generated for the census figures, it was still true that large numbers of peasants had been removed from the land. By the census of 1710, many peasants had been conscripted and lay dead at Narva and Lesnaya and Poltava, and many others waited in dread for the coming campaign on the distant Pruth. Still others had been mobilized for labor gangs at Taganrog, Voronezh, Smolensk, or Petersburg. And still others, fewer in number but hardier in spirit, had taken their families and fled their lands and their heavy obligations to find a new life in the Cossack lands of the steppe or across the Urals into Siberia.

A suggestion much discussed in preceding reigns and developed into a proposal in the regency of Sophia was a poll tax, a tax on individuals. Peter seized upon the idea without a full realization of all its implications. The Tsar was no economist but he had strong feelings about state service and saw this as an opportunity to implement the concept on a wide scale among the lower classes of his realm. A poll tax also promised major solutions to the problems revealed by the census of 1710. This tax was implemented by the census of 1718 on nearly the entire male population of Muscovy; all male "souls" of whatever age, except those belonging to the privileged nobility and clergy, were included. The census thereby dragged in under its simple classifications of private serf and state peasant many groups not previously covered by the household tax. The "revisions" of the census in 1721 and again in 1724 brought the total of male "souls" to 5.5 million. The divisions of these taxable persons showed 78 per cent as privately owned serfs, 19 per cent as state-owned peasants, and 3 per cent as town dwellers. An insight into Peter's purposes and methods is provided by the allocation of the income from the poll tax and the technique of its formulation: the poll tax was directed to cover the total of military expenditures and its sum was arrived at by dividing those military costs by the number of available taxpayers. The system was meant to finance the costly war effort on a "pay as you go" basis.

The results were substantial: the household tax had brought in about 1 million rubles in 1681 and the poll tax raised that figure to about 4.5 million rubles in 1724. Peter was able to leave his state without substantial debt, an astonishing legacy most uncommon among his fellow monarchs. At the same time, the poll tax tended to increase the land being put into cultivation: since a man was no longer taxed by the household but by the head, the more land he could put into cultivation the higher his income, while his tax remained the same. The households which had amalgamated and retrenched under earlier legislation now spread and proliferated under the new. This was important to Petrine Russia, since increased agricultural productivity in the eighteenth century came only from expanding the land in use.

Still the poll tax had severe consequences in Muscovite society, for not by bread alone do governments live. The burden laid upon individual peasants by Peter was radically increased because most males on the tax rolls were not really self-supporting; the able-bodied men of the family had to make up the burdens of the children, the aged, and the ill. "At one stroke he swept into oblivion the old Muscovite concept that taxes should be based upon ability to pay." [3] The poll tax was also a substantial monument in the history of Russian serfdom, although no one at the Petrine court would ever have so recognized it. The census for the poll tax and its subsequent revisions simply ignored all legal gradations of bonded peasants and even slaves; it amalgamated them into a body of serfs to whom one simple law could apply by the simple expedient of requiring all forms of the peasantry to register for tax purposes with private landlords, state peasant communities, or the army. This extension of serfdom to many formerly distinct categories, largely by indirection, was the product of a war reformer in a hurry: all projects are to be judged by the simplicity with which they can be effected, by the minimum cost they will require, and by the immediacy of the results they will engender. It was not to the advantage of the state to distinguish varieties of peasants and varieties of taxes. Nor was it to the advantage of the state to be forced to create a costly body of civil servants in local government to minister to such distinctions. There was no tax farm-

[3] Jerome Blum, *Lord and Peasant in Russia From the Ninth to the Nineteenth Century* (New York: Atheneum Publishers, 1964), p. 463.

ing as in the French system, no ability to institute a numerous salaried local bureaucracy, and no desire, as evidence the gap in the last provincial reform, to permit the peasants to tax themselves. At first, the army was charged with the collection of the poll tax, but the ultimate logic required that landlords be the primary census takers and tax gatherers, which would cost the state nothing in money but a great deal in effective authority, and would cost the peasant the last remnant of his freedom. A serf not only lost more of his income to the state but, far from reaping greater benefits therefrom, at the same time lost state protection against the arbitrary hold of the land-lord over his life.

Indirect taxation may have given way in importance under Peter but it still occupied a substantial place in Muscovite state revenues. The Tsar Peter employed a group of advisers whose function was to dream up new sources of such revenues. The usual recourse of these brain trusters was to search out another product or another service which had not yet been taxed, and from one end of Muscovy to the other the list of such items grew: on beards, Old Believers, coach services, public documents, articles of clothing, hearths, rented rooms, baths, beehives, ice blocks, sunflower seeds, birth registration, flour mills, and even on non-Orthodox marriages. In the same spirit the government expanded its traditional trade monopolies, reserving to itself the heavy profit from liquor sales, from the vast and vital salt trade, and from the sales of furs, fish oil, tobacco, caviar, coffins, and even rhubarb. The state liquor stores, especially, struck a happy profit. The burdens of these indirect taxes were heavy and caused rumblings of discontent as they multiplied. They might in fact be more disturb-ing than direct taxes, for they struck daily at the necessities of life. It will be seen that not even the Church escaped the financial roundup, for in 1700 the Tsar began the diversion of monastery incomes to war needs.

If the experiments in administration were designed to develop larger revenues and to improve the flow of funds as well as to implement the will of the monarch more efficiently, these tasks were surely dependent on a supply of manpower sufficient in numbers and quality to under-take them. Expanded central offices in the Senate and in the Colleges, new provincial posts, new diplomatic and commercial assignments abroad, more numerous commands in the army and navy, all made demands for men—the bureaucracy needed bureaucrats. And this need could not simply be filled by the crude conscription which served the army's basic needs. The men required for the new administration would not only require basic literacy but, ultimately, the command of foreign languages and the ability to care for the complex accounts of a modern state. The manpower pool for this new administrative and financial structure was of necessity the Muscovite nobility who would have to be organized, trained, supported, and infused with a new spirit. Moving the nobility into the administrative structure would reshape their role in history; surely no more than that need be said to demonstrate that administrative reforms may sometimes assist in the reworking of society in unexpected ways.

☸ 5 ☸

Aristocrat and Serf

One of the most important tasks in the building of the centralized absolute monarchies of early modern Europe was the staffing of their bureaucracies. A ruler by the grace of God, armies, or Hobbesian necessity, was still but a single man initiating and then struggling with ever larger and more complex tasks. It was soon apparent to such monarchs that they were really no more powerful and successful than their civil servants were talented, efficient, dedicated, disciplined, and increased in numbers. The solution of each European monarchy to this central problem depended strongly upon its individual inheritance, and the solution in each case had an immense amount to do with the future of the state. For Louis XIV, for example, that eternal lighter-than-air phenomenon of American college lectures, the rising bourgeoisie, provided a talented manpower pool from which the monarch might draw administrators and thus avoid dependence on the jealous aristocracy; this solution had profound and unforeseen consequences. The Great Elector of Brandenburg, on the other hand, pursued the transformation of the junker landowners into a hereditary service class with similarly significant effects. The Polish monarchy, to choose an example from the opposite end of the spectrum, never undertook to exert its will and build a bureaucracy to implement it, and neither the monarchy nor Poland survived the competition with states that did. The problems posed by major European warfare and its concomitant government reorganizations were, therefore, not peculiar to Muscovy. Peter and his fellow "pragmatic" monarchs were in search of a large, trainable body of military and civil servants to staff their armies and administrations. For Peter there was no burgeoning middle class as in France; the Tsar might have dreamed secret dreams of the options available to Louis XIV, but his inheritance, for all of its difficulties, was still the Muscovite nobility.

Peter was also equipped for his task with a principle at once Muscovite and generally European—the principle of state service. It is true enough that the idea that the nobility of the Muscovite Tsardom owed service to its Tsar in return for its lands dated from the days of Ivan III and may well have been an adaptation of Tatar practice. But it was also true that the principle of state service was in the European air, radiated by the likes of Richelieu and the Grand Elector to rationalize and legalize the end of dynastic and regional loyalties and the creation of stronger ties to the state. Recall, if you will, Peter's message to his troops at Poltava which told the army "that it must not think of itself as formed to fight for Peter, but for the Russian Tsardom entrusted to Peter by his birth and by the all-Russian people." It has even been said that the Tsar called himself "the first servant of the state." A contrast of such vocabulary with the oft-quoted comment of Louis XIV, "l'état, c'est moi," might suggest that Peter had a more modern view of the state than did the Sun King. Peter would therefore implement those principles which could be adapted practically to his needs by imposing service on all classes, high and low. That service fell most conspicuously on the nobles and most heavily on the peasants of Muscovy.

If Peter was plagued by needs and armed with principles derived from his Muscovite inheritance and the European climate, that did not mean that the Muscovite nobility was ready to cooperate in meeting those needs and implementing those principles. The general run of the nobility resisted Peter and strenuously so. Most Muscovite nobles, and even the terms "noble" and "nobility" are unsatisfactory before Peter, had no tradition whatever of doing the dreary work of civil administration, nor did they even see their military obligations in anything like a Petrine way. The vaunted Muscovite heritage of state service was for the bulk of the nobles only the traditional necessity of defending the land in moments of extreme crisis because they could not really avoid it, and then they were accustomed to performing this service in their own territories and under their own leaders. Their traditions did not include their own education, any active role in local government, any attempt to institutionalize their position, or any promotion of the general welfare. It was customary for the nobility in general to shirk their service obligations as often as possible, especially after the Polish menace had subsided in the seventeenth century. In the words of the merchant Pososhkov, "they care nothing about killing the enemy but care only about returning to their homes. . . . They pray that God send them a light wound so as not to suffer much . . . and I have even heard noblemen say 'Pray God we may serve our sovereign without drawing our swords from their scabbards.' "

By 1700 the Muscovite nobility appeared in two rather distinct service groups. The metropolitan nobles of Moscow were really the model of Peter's reforms and the bane of his existence at the same time. The Metropolitan nobility was composed of families which had settled in Moscow and its suburbs since its expansion in the fourteenth century, including "mediatized" or transferred princes from Lithuania, the conquered Tatar khanates, and the old Kievan lands; and Muscovite *pomestie* familes settled around Moscow by the Tsar's orders to ensure his protection, largely in the time of Ivan the Terrible. These families provided the personnel for the working and ceremonial offices which ran old Muscovy. They were the members and the staff of the *Boya Duma* and the *prikazi*, the ambassadors and special legates, the governors of the provinces, and even the military commanders who took the field commands in the system of precedence to provide adequate leadership for the convened feudal levies of the provincials. For them, military and civil service were one, and the prerogative of their families in perpetuity.

These serving families lived on the donation of the Tsar, holding grants of estates and serfs in the environs of Moscow and increasing their wealth by accumulating more distant holdings, which they seldom visited, also by grant from the Tsar. They thought of themselves as the social betters of the backward landowners in the provinces; as a matter of fact, they would not have admitted any mutuality of origin, interest, or function with the backward provincials. It was this group which produced those families and individuals most prone to assist the Tsar in his programs of centralization, so long as the primary role was theirs. From their ranks came men whose eyes and ears were open to the rest of Europe, and from them came even some of Peter's original toy troops, provincial governors, ambassadors, and military commanders. One problem plagued the metropolitan nobles: they might have been satisfactory to run old Muscovy but they were not sufficient in numbers nor yet in training to run a modern state in the throes of a major war and of administrative expansion. Unfortunately for the Tsar, but naturally enough for them, they were extremely jealous of their role, insistent on their rights, and confirmed in their resistance to an influx of outsiders into their ranks.

The second group of nobles was by far the larger, and calling them provincial nobility ought not to obscure the fact that some of them lived in the neighborhood of urban centers such as Kiev, Smolensk, Archangel, or Kazan, and would willingly come to Moscow when called to do their duty in crisis or to accept special assignment in return for grants of lands. But by far the majority of the nobility hated service in the terms described by Pososhkov. They skirted their obligations whenever possible, they resisted training, they complained and wept when they were hounded out to do their duties. Many of these "nobles" lived hidden away in the provinces, with the government in Moscow almost completely ignorant of their numbers, or location, or the type of their land tenure, or the state of their well-being. In 1690, for example, the bulk of these "nobles" each controlled considerably less than twenty male serfs, while only twelve landowners in all of Muscovy owned more than one thousand peasant households. It was to this group of provincials that Peter turned to staff the new Russia, and it was his intent to "metropolitanize" the whole nobility in order to meet his needs.

Peter's first step in organizing his nobility was taken in 1700 when he ordered all landowners to notify the *Prikaz* of War of the numbers and location of all nobles over ten years old. This decree and its implementation bordered on a conscription, since Peter, in addition simply to determining the size and whereabouts of his service class, also immediately began to distribute the registrants into regiments, into posts in the civil service, and even into groups being sent overseas for study. It was usual for Peter himself to question members of the nobility, to determine their abilities, and to make their assignments. Peter did not have good luck with this decree, and the years after 1700 saw Pososhkov's analysis demonstrated in practice: the nobles struggled to ignore their activist Tsar.

A decree of 1714 brought the weight of the new government to bear on the nobility; all nobles would immediately enroll with the newly created Senate or face the confiscation of their property, on the principle that they all owed service for their land and otherwise ought not to hold it. Despite harsh punishments added for failure to enroll, including even outlawry by 1722, the problem of avoidance was continual. The chief device of the nobility for eluding service, testifying to human ingenuity, was to pretend insanity. Peter, responding with equal ingenuity, decreed that any noble registered as insane would be forbidden to marry or to inherit.

A decree of 1722 instituted the office of *Heraldmeister,* which was attached to the All-Governing Senate; to this officer was delegated all matters relating to the nobility, with especial responsibility for maintaining their fitness and availability for service. The *Heraldmeister* was to keep a register of all nobles and a current list of all their male children and their dates of birth; he was also to maintain a school of economics and government training and to insure that the less onerous burdens of the civil service were not selected by more than one third of any single aristocratic family. This last injunction is revealing, first of Peter's preference for the military over the civil service and of the truly military nature of Russian society, and second of the fact that before Peter, the Muscovite nobility was not all that militaristic. The prestige and attraction of the military for the Russian aristocracy in the centuries to come was largely Peter's contribution.

Registration was but the beginning. As the army increased in number and expanded its techniques and as the offices of the new administration proliferated and became more specialized, it was absolutely necessary that those obliged to serve be trained for their tasks. The decree of 1714 set the beginning of noble service at age fifteen, but the decree was quite specific in demanding preliminary schooling: "The Great Sovereign decrees that in all provinces the children between ten and fifteen of the nobility, of government clerks, and of lessor officials, except those of freeholders, must be taught mathematics and geometry." Schools were to be established at churches and monasteries in every province, to be staffed by graduates of the Moscow Mathematics College, which had been founded in 1703.

The preliminary schooling introduced an important new element into Muscovite life. Secular education had been unheard of in Muscovy; education of the young had been restricted to the clergy and to the sons of the very wealthy nobility and was completely controlled by the Church in personnel and curriculum. It must be admitted, however, that Petrine concepts of education were completely bound up with state service requirements rather than with any general dedication to the "enlightening" function of knowledge; he was seeking qualified bureaucrats and not candidates for the French Academy. It must also be admitted that Peter's educational reform was the least effective of any, and that these schools were not opened in the provinces in any numbers, thanks to the diversion of funds to war and other related tasks and to the unwillingness of the Church to co-operate in any such venture. Nor did the provision for a compulsory educational system necessarily inspire its students to use it. Peter's attempts to provide schools for noble sons was matched by a more successful attempt of the sons to stay away from them. Parents held knowledge to be the road to heresy or the means by which their sons would be torn from them and even dispatched into infected foreign lands. Peter reacted by insisting that no young noble could marry unless he had a certificate of mathematics qualification at age fifteen, and actually punished notorious truants by assigning them to manual labor on the foundations of Saint Petersburg.

After preliminary education the nobles who enlisted in state service at age fifteen theoretically started at the bottom rung of either the civil or military service in a form of "on-the-job training." Clerks in the civil service were to learn their duties from the ground up and officers in the army were to serve two years in the ranks before re-ceiving their commissions, a practice continued until 1716. The only escape from such duty was enrollment in the Tsar's Guards Regiments, which in 1719 added a third, the Life Regiment of Dragoons, in which all members, from enlisted men through officers, were nobles. Nobles naturally aspired to avoid two years in the ranks for their sons by having them enrolled in the Guards; Peter was thus able to reward those who cooperated with him by granting appointments in these prestige units. Thus, historians have pointed out the vital importance of these all-noble regiments to the development of an aristocratic class consciousness and solidarity. Despite the relatively small num-bers of the Guards, about 3,000, these havens provided the aristocracy, and most especially the provincial aristocracy who had enjoyed little share in state power before Peter, with an instrument of power close to the throne; the Guards would represent their group interests force-fully in the century to come. Peter had no intentions of creating a political force out of the Guards, but history is paved with "no in-tentions."

The conditions of service for the aristocracy were burdensome. In the eighteenth century the nobility would demand relief from some of the more onerous of the Petrine burdens even after they had accepted the main outlines of his reform. The primary complaint against Petrine service was its lifetime tenure. When the Great Northern War was concluded nobles were promised a six-month leave every two years in order to take some stock of their estates, but the war lasted twenty years. Retirement from service was reserved to the wounded, the aged, and the incompetent, and even these, including the last category, would be assigned to local garrison duty. Indeed, manpower demands were so great that even Swedish prisoners of war found themselves in government posts. Life service meant that estates were left for most of the time in the hands of women, peasant stewards, or incompetent relatives, and this usually meant in turn that noble estates were badly managed and unproductive. This life service also accustomed the noble to be separated from his land even though he resisted it in the first generation, and accustomed him as well to city life and its joys. In this sense, life service was but one more force separating the new nobility from the rural life of Muscovy.

The new service conditions also established the primacy of the military over all other branches. It had been the custom of pre-Petrine Muscovy to mingle civil and military duty in the same leadership, but the modern demands of war and government made this impossible. Peter could allow no choice between the two forms of service, for all his enforced nobles would have chosen the easier life of the civil servant; the decree of the *Heraldmeister* on limiting one third of any family to civil service was evidence enough. Peter helped to transform this aristocratic penchant by himself insisting on the primacy and honor of military appointment. He paid great honor to officers, and permitted no comparison of civil and military ranks in social situations by indicating that an officer, no matter what his grade, was the social equal of any civil servant no matter how elevated. To the discomfort of his civil service, Peter personally relied on favorite members of the guards to accomplish many tasks for him, including the supervision of the Senate and special embassies abroad. The military caste of mind of the nobility in the much-uniformed nineteenth century owed much to Peter, as did the militarist characters of such emperors as Peter III, Paul, Alexander I, and Nicholas I. To be a "simple soldier" was the greatest Russian service.

The most striking innovation in Petrine service was the Table of Ranks which was decreed in 1722 to concretize the practice of the Tsar. Mechanically, the Table worked simply; it divided government service into three branches of army, navy, and civil service and established fourteen ranks in each branch. The word for a rank on the Table was *chin*, a Tatar word from whence *chinovnik*, the word for bureaucrat. The fourteen ranks began with the lowliest task in each branch (collegiate registrar, gunnery officer, guidon bearer) and rose to the highest (Chancellor or Active Privy Counselor, General-Admiral, Generalissimo, or Field Marshal.) The decree clearly stated the theory behind the Table: to replace an inherited hierarchy based on birth and wealth with a bureaucratic hierarchy based on talent. "Although we permit free entry to public assemblies where the court is present to the sons of . . . high state servants . . . we nevertheless do not grant any ranks to anyone until he performs a useful service to us. . . ." The lowest six ranks conferred personal nobility and the eight highest ranks granted hereditary nobility and rank equal to the most ancient families of the realm. This was the new dispensation toward which the seventeenth century had been drifting: aristocracy dependent upon rank rather than rank dependent upon aristocracy.

There is some small argument about the role of this Table of Ranks in producing a physical expansion of the Russian nobility. If one takes seriously the vague statistics which indicate about 3,000 noble families in 1670 and about 100,000 noble families in 1737, then some explanation must be provided. The historian Vasili Klyuchevsky leaned to the "democratic" interpretation of the Table, maintaining that the scheme opened the door of the aristocracy to men of talent;[1] *pomeshchiks* of old had been chosen and patronized in a similar manner to offset the influence of the hereditary nobility. Professor Paul Miliukov, however, emphasized that the Table of Ranks was intended to winnow out and promote the most talented in the nobility and not necessarily the most talented in the state; he held that noble bloodlines and prior registration with the *Heraldmeister* were generally required before one could even put his foot on the first rank and try to demonstrate capacity enough to rise higher.[2] If non-noble families appeared in the Table, it was largely because registration of noble families was haphazard, and was therefore accidental rather than planned. Miliukov would admit general ennobling of lower classes only on the military side, where Peter very clearly decreed that those receiving officers' commissions were indeed entitled to noble status; the number of these could not have been great. The general disposition of Peter to act within the limits of his century would tend to support Miliukov, even though individuals such as the Demidovs of the mining industry were

[1] Vasili Klyuchevsky, *Peter the Great*, trans. Liliana Archibald (New York: St. Martin's Press, 1963), pp. 100–101.

[2] P. Miliukov, C. Seignobos, and L. Eisenmann, *Histoire de Russie* (Paris: Ernest Leroux, 1932), I, 391–92.

rewarded with noble status for their services to the state. But most such cases of ennobling were created directly by the Tsar and were not "earned" through the Table of Ranks. The expanded figures for the Russian aristocracy would then be largely explained by the stringency of Peter's registration requirements after 1700, which reflected reality more accurately than did the statistics of 1670.

The table of Ranks clearly established in law the Petrine distinction between civil and military service, and in the process certainly contributed to the establishment of the bureaucratic image so much abused in the next century. The Table also presumed a basic education not required or provided for the rest of the society, which signalled the separation of the nobility from their ancient culture. At the same time the Table ignored the territorial basis of service and thereby moved toward the removal of the nobility from their provincial ties. Further, the metropolitan and the provincial gentry were now mixed together in one service class; the old metropolitan nobility who had charged themselves with control of Muscovy were inundated and submerged in a new national bureaucracy. The metropolitan nobles bridled at the Tsar's instruction that "members of ancient noble families, even though they be of lesser status and never before treated with noble dignity by the Crown . . . shall be given the same merits and preferences as others." This unified nobility was described by a new name, *shliakhetstvo*, drawn from the Polish. Finally, the Table of Ranks never did represent more than a guide and an ideal. Peter himself was the main violator of the principle of promotion by trial and talent. Surrounded by deception, corruption, stupidity, and stubbornness, he continued to patronize his friends, to promote his comrades at his whim, and to prefer the favorites in the Guards to carry on much of his business. The old maxim of the seventeenth century, that the road to power was the friendship of the Tsar, still held firm.

An enrolled, semi-educated, and articulated civil service still required to be supported, and that for an early-eighteenth-century government was the most severe test of all. Driven by the necessity for financing armies, diplomacy, and the national economy, monarchs were hardpressed to pay their servants. This simple fact explains why Peter did not alter but rather intensified the granting of estates and the expansion of serfdom. Serfdom was the condition which, as in the difficult recovery during the seventeenth century, enabled the ruler to enjoy the military services of a self-supporting nobility. Still, state servants were only as useful as the success of the economic structure which supported them, and the Muscovite nobility in Peter's day was in severe difficulties.

Peter was studying a decree in which *votchina* and *pomestie* tenure, inherited and service estates, would be melded legally into a system of inherited estates, all of which would bear service requirements. But it was the problem of inheritance which bothered Peter most. He could see that *votchina* holders of the seventeenth century had often lost their status and come begging for grants of estates because Muscovite testamentary practice was completely on the side of the division of estates among all male heirs. For the same reason, service estates had been so reduced in size as to be worthless as support. If such practices continued, nobles with service obligations would not hold enough land to keep them above abject poverty, and poverty-stricken bureaucrats were of no use to the state. Some reform of inheritance practices was required, and Peter had been collecting evidence on the problem from all parts of Europe.

In a decree of March, 1714, Peter established the permanent union of inherited property and service obligation, and at the same time issued new regulations on testaments because "the division of estates at the father's death causes great harm to the state and its interests and brings ruin to subjects and to the families concerned." The rules were simple: estates could not be sold out of the family so that a family would have no material support for its service obligations, and estates were to be bequeathed to only one selected son although the "movables" of an estate could be allotted among all the heirs. This is called a law of "entail" and not "primogeniture," since Peter required that the land be passed intact to any son and not necessarily the eldest.

Peter enumerated many subsidiary reasons for this decree. It was hoped that it would indirectly benefit the Russian peasantry, since Peter saw heavier and heavier burdens from more and more owners on less and less property if the old practice continued. Such increased demands from more landlords on small estates could only damage the tax-paying abilities of the peasantry. It was also thought that those sons of the nobility who did not share in the inheritance "will not be idle because they will be forced to earn a living through service, teaching, commerce, and so forth." The decree insisted that no dishonor would attach to such sons who went into trade or industry, "so that cadets might seek their own bread through some service." It was also intended that the law of entail would promote the status of the *shliakhetstvo* by assuring that its members were land- and serf-owners of guaranteed prosperity who would not be permitted to fall into poverty and shame.

This aspect of the Petrine reform of the aristocracy was the least permanent, for the Empress Anne repealed the law of entail in 1730. The old Muscovite practice triumphed over the dead Tsar, as the new Empress confirmed that it was "contrary to God's justice" to separate some children from their inheritance. It was also explained that estate owners would hand over the movables of the estate, consisting of tools, plows, wagons, and animals, to the other sons, effectively rendering the estate worthless. Even worse, many dispossessed sons became dependent on their relatives, living upon the estates like drones or traveling about Europe at the estate's expense.

Despite the repeal of the law of entail, something substantial had happened as a result of its enactment. It ended once and for all the old distinctions between inherited and service estates, and conferred on the Russian nobles as a class for the first time the absolute right to ownership of their lands and the peoples upon them. The aristocracy was in the process of cementing its hold on Russia for the coming century. The peasantry was now subjugated in law to the control of an inherited family rather than some theoretically transitory *pomeshchik* who stood over their lives only as a temporary substitute for the Father-Tsar. Such a legal establishment of seventeenth-century practice certainly strengthened the theoretical foundations of the Russian aristocracy and certainly dealt a vicious blow to the peasant's traditional view of his place. The peasants were aware of the fact that they were now considered the property of the noble, while they considered themselves the children of the Tsar. This change has much to do with the severe peasant revolts in this century.

As is obvious from even this discussion of the law of entail, despite the stubbornness of the aristocracy and their struggle against the Petrine decrees, and despite the weak development of some aspects of the reform, the aristocratic decrees had major consequences. The *shliakhetstvo* had been transported from their provinces and enrolled in service far from the peasants with whom they had formerly much in common. They were gathered into groups where they could not help but identify with their common interests, and the Guards regiments were the best example. They were thrown into situations, especially in the new city of Petersburg and in western Europe, where they could not avoid becoming more urban, more cosmopolitan, more attuned to the manners and intellectual fashions of international Europe, and consequently, less responsive to the values of the rural life they had reluctantly left behind. The nobility was, in short, being forced to become an aristocracy, and became addicted to the power, the influence, income, standard of living, and styles of life which for much of Peter's reign they had inveighed against so bitterly. The sons whose fathers had fought so desperately to save their "darling boys" from the wayward ways of Paris or the German spas were themselves sending their sons there and making their own comfortable way in the rest of Europe.

In the process of the reforms the newly coalesced *shliakhetstvo* had altered their relationship to their ruler as well. It is usual to read in general texts that Peter bound the nobility to state service and brought them under the ruler's control. Such a summary view was only temporarily true. By 1725 the nobles were hardly *kholopi* or slaves of the Tsar any longer, and hence that Muscovite term passed out of use. They filled the government and military posts, ran the embassies, oversaw commercial and industrial development, governed the provinces, and presided in complete autonomy over their lands and serfs; the Petrine state could not exist without them. Peter had created a government and handed it over to his aristocracy. If European monarchs in general became in part limited by their bureaucracies in the eighteenth century, then surely the Russian ruler was a prime example, and if the eighteenth century witnessed a general aristocratic resurgence, then never was the ground better prepared than in Russia. The *generalitet*, or eight highest ranks of the service, were in the indispensable agents of the Tsar's will. The Russian nobility in 1725 found itself not only permanently subverted by "European" culture but forcibly charged with control of a great state. What they had fought so hard to resist in Peter's reign they defended with devotion for the rest of the century.

Whatever his complaints about service in Peter's reign, the aristocrat was paid rather well for his unwilling cooperation. The peasant performed far heavier and more onerous service in the military, in forced labor gangs, and in the taxation and agricultural services which increased threefold in his lifetime; and for all his service to the Petrine system he received nothing at all. It is far simpler than summarizing the aristocratic reform, then, to summarize the "short and simple annals of the poor." In the work of the merchant Pososhkov, *On Poverty and Wealth,* he synopsized the life of the Petrine peasant as an unhappy mixture of tyranny, overwork, drink, crowded homes, fires, blights, banditry, illiteracy, and extortion.

The Russian peasants lived isolated in their villages; the nineteenth-century Russian revolutionary Alexander Herzen described them as "that *magnum ignotum,* that people—muted, poor, semi-barbarous— which concealed itself in its villages, behind the snow, behind bad roads, only appearing in the streets of Saint Petersburg like a foreign outcast, with its persecuted beard and prohibited dress—tolerated only through contempt." And those peasant villages were far distant from twentieth-century daydreams about rural communities; they were small, squalid collections of mud huts within whose dank precincts the families from elders to children gathered in concentric rings of precedence around the life-giving stove. Here the laws on beards and clothes penetrated only vaguely and here the foreign fashions of Petersburg were seen only during the summer visits of the serving gentry; the peasants themselves wore their homespun blouses, shaggy sheepskin jackets, and baggy trousers, and wrapped their feet in cloth for the cruel winters or shuffled in bark sandals. Here came no news of distant Amsterdam or London, no plays fresh from the Paris stage; here rather the small church staffed by its priests no richer and no more educated than the peasants themselves served their souls and their bodies through their short and narrow lives; existence revolved around three recurring rituals of birth, marriage, and death. But, with all such miseries understood, the reader must guard against his own disposition to think of peasants as ever striving to forsake their rural ties and make their way into cosmopolitan city life; peasants were attached to their land above all else, and could draw the little satis-faction their lives allowed them from the terms of seventeenth-century serfdom which at least guaranteed them in their tenure.

It was in the grain fields that the peasants spent the bulk of their lives and in which they struggled to manage their heavy burdens. Nature treated them even more dreadfully than it did their western-European counterparts; autumns were unpredictable, winters were deep and bitter, springs were drowned in mud, and summers were hot and dry. Peasant obligations were double; they paid their taxes to the crown through their landlords, and they paid their obligations to their landlords either in goods or cash where they worked their own land exclusively or in labor where the landlord kept some land for his own production; and this double burden to state and landlord rose constantly during the seventeenth and eighteenth centuries. The peasants worked as did their fathers before them and pulled their own plows if they were not prosperous enough to have an animal. If the bureaucracy in Petersburg was "modernizing" its structure and the gentry was "modernizing" its life style, no hint of movement was really observable in the tilled fields of Russia.

The peasants were being pushed more and more toward communal forms of organization, forms favored by the state because they guaranteed a general level of taxpaying ability. The pressures of the poll tax were significant in this regard. Taxation and conscription, for example, could be allotted first by government to landlord and then by landlord to the elders of the village community, or *mir*. The community itself might then distribute its own tax burdens or conscriptions to its own families with a form of rough justice and equality. Land, too, might be repartitioned periodically by communities in some areas to guarantee fair treatment to families, making it necessary for all families to plow together, sow together, cultivate and harvest together. While nineteenth-century romantics would make much of the virtues of this communal peasant life, the peasants themselves struggled against these emerging practices, of the eighteenth century which discouraged initiative and rewarded mediocrity.

The peasant's attitude toward his government was doubly disturbed. On the one hand, the government was the agency which ordered his conscription; no peasant parting for twenty-five years of service in the army could reasonably expect to see his family again. He was forced to fight in distant climes for advantages quite unclear to him and for a Tsar who seemed more a foreigner than an all-protecting father. If the peasant escaped the annual harvesting of troops, he might just as easily find himself ordered to the distant Don or to Ingria on some labor project. And if he were a state peasant who escaped either conscription, perhaps he might be honored by a trip to the Urals for "temporary" work in the mines and forges, or find his village purchased by some strange industry. If by some incredible stroke of fortune he survived all these attentions, he could be certain that the burden of taxes would grow incessantly and that the new poll tax would ignore his privileges and customary distinctions and lump him and all his cohorts across the land into one desperate serfdom.

On the other hand, the government attitude toward the peasant's plight was one of withdrawal. The government might physically withdraw, as in the case of state peasants handed over to private landlords or to industrial interests. But the government also withdrew philosophically from the protection of the peasants, handing their fate over completely to the landlords. It might have been a necessity for a government which was financially hard pressed to avoid creating a vast new provincial bureaucracy to administer the peasantry, and simply to invest the landlords with the authority to tax, conscript, and keep order. But the peasant could only see that the rightful duty of the Tsar, to watch over and protect God's people, had been ceded away to miserable landlords who did not carry their responsibility from God. The merchant Pososhkov pleaded in vain that "not the nobles but the Tsar must protect the peasants because the nobles control them for a while, while the Tsar keeps them eternally."

It was the duty of the Tsar, as Ivan the Terrible had defined it and as the Time of Troubles had confirmed, to mediate between classes, to prevent one group in the society from preying upon the others. In the words of Ivan, "rulers themselves, and not the boyars and not the notables, must govern the entire realm." But Peter's government convinced the peasants beyond doubt of their seventeenth-century suspicions, that the Tsar had forfeited his duty to govern the entire realm and had become the partisan of the landowner. And the peasant also knew, in a simple but nonetheless accurate fashion, that a radical change had taken place in land tenure. It was a peasant maxim that "the land is ours and we are the Tsar's," a formulation from which mention of the aristocrat is conspicuously absent. Landlords were temporary evils, borne because the Tsar needed their help in crisis; *pomestie* tenure might have been burdensome, but it preserved in theory the temporary quality of the landlord and the eternal relationship of peasant and Tsar. But now all that had been changed, and lands and peoples were recognized as the property of the landlord. God's Tsar had abandoned his people; was it any wonder that God had abandoned the Tsar?

It is not difficult, then, to see why the peasantry in general and the Old Believers in particular among them were dismayed by the policies of the state. It had attacked them in the two properties they held most dear—their faith and their land. They were forbidden to worship in the ancient manner of their fathers and forbidden to live quietly in their homes; they were made as close to slaves as the modern era has come. They could not call up the abstractions nor command the vocabulary to label the Tsar as the agent of the new state absolutism which required their complete subjection to its service, but they could

find labels such as "Satan" and "Antichrist," titles perhaps more ap-
plicable to the modern absolute state than many would like, in nerv-
ousness, to admit. Russian peasants developed feelings toward the
state which ranged from patient suffering to vicious hatred. And the
reaction of the Tsar and his advisers to such growing murmurs and
complaints was simple: to lay upon the society a layer of agents to
listen everywhere for rebellious "word or deed" against the Tsar and
to crush them viciously wherever they were found.

The peasant reaction to Peter's reforms ultimately produced more
than spiritual fear or philosophical anxiety. The simplest response was
to run away. The southern Cossack lands of the Dnieper, the Don, and
the Ural attracted many, and there is just cause for seeing Peter's
campaigns in the south as partly designed to close these drains. Certainly the autonomy of the Dnieper Cossacks was ended and peasants
were forced farther into the southern Urals and into Siberia to find
any peace from the hounding state. Flight ultimately welled into rebellion, at Astrakhan in 1706, among the Cossacks in 1707, and in the
valley of the Volga almost continually. It serves as a healthy antidote
to the western European view of the Russian peasantry, raised too
exclusively on Dostoievsky, as spiritually deep and patiently suffering
in its misery, to be reminded of the continual peasant unrest of the
late seventeenth and eighteenth centuries which periodically launched
vast popular upheavals of incredible violence. But more of this opposition later.

Peter, then, hastened the development of the Russian aristocracy
and handed over to it the beginnings of a workable state machinery,
and at the same time he completed the subjection of the bulk of his
subjects to the control of that aristocracy. Aristocrats were granted
privileges and responsibilities, which responsibilities they would soon
abandon; peasants were saddled only with responsibilities, and those
they could not abandon without bringing down both state and landlords.

Peter left the mass of the Russian population in far more miserable
condition than he found them. Historians have claimed beneficial
effects in every area of his reforms, but none has ever tried to salvage
Peter as even a minor benefactor of the peasantry. But one may
wonder whether it is more profitable to heap blame on Peter for this
failure or to attempt to understand it. Peter as the benefactor of the
peasantry would have been an astonishing anachronism in his age. In

every part of Europe the reforms of army and administration were direct, while effects for good or ill upon the peasantry were indirect and derivative; no monarch anywhere yet conceived the public welfare as much more than the taxpaying capability of his subjects. But while it is important to see the Russian peasant problem in the perspective of European monarchs, it is even more important to see its peculiarity. In western Europe, for reasons with which the monarchs had little to do, serfdom was a dying institution. It was still strong in Holstein and in parts of north Germany, and survived even in parts of France, but it was a medieval pattern rapidly losing ground before new forces. In Russia, however, serfdom was a relatively new institution which received strong impetus from the reconquest of the seventeenth century. It was a far stronger force to stem in Muscovy than in most states of western Europe precisely because it was tied up with rather than divorced from state institutions. Serfdom supported the service nobility, which grew more and more important through the seventeenth century and into Peter's reign, and insured the availability of the population for taxation and conscription at minimum cost. Peter had few flights of historical imagination and usually hewed rather rigorously to innovations of his given heritage; and therefore Peter would never have considered or even have found an alternative to serfdom as the support of his service nobility and the best guarantee of popular contributions to his work. One wonders if the Petrine reforms would have been possible without the subjection of the peasantry which they involved.

But Peter, please remember, was not the last Russian Emperor but the first. It is hardly fair for historians to avoid explanations of the failure of leadership of his successors by fatalistically tying the peasant problem of the nineteenth century and even the Bolshevik revolution directly to Tsar Peter. Peter was an eighteenth-century ruler working within his inheritance and within the political and social limits of his age. It was sufficient unto the day for Peter to push forward the amalgamation of the aristocracy, for, to quote Professor R. R. Palmer's comment on the Russian aristocracy at the end of the eighteenth century, "for some to have a sphere of rights due to special birth or rank was doubtless better than for no one to have any assured rights at all." [3] No one can minimize the severe limitations which the peasant

[3] R. R. Palmer, *The Age of the Democratic Revolution: The Challenge* (Princeton: Princeton University Press, 1959), p. 404.

problem imposed on governments to come, for Peter had completed its incorporation into the fabric of the Russian system. What is offered here is not an excuse but an explanation and a concluding evasion; truly the immense legacy of the peasant problem, as it was in all parts of Europe, was really the business of another age.

❇ 6 ❇

Commerce and Industry

We have become accustomed to think of old Russia as "underdeveloped," a favorite word of our times, and we have become just as accustomed to think of its corollary, of old Russia coming into contact with "European" or "western" economic development and struggling against medieval obstacles to reach its level of attainment. The pontification of Joseph Stalin provided a classic formulation: "When Peter the Great, having relations with the developed countries of the west, feverishly built mills and factories for the supply of his army and the strengthening of the country's defense, this was an original attempt to escape from the framework of backwardness." But, as several perceptive historians have recently reminded us, there was not one "Europe" but many, and not one "western tradition" but several. If England and the Netherlands were the leaders in ocean-borne commerce in the late seventeenth century, then surely Russia was backward in relation to them in those areas; but then so were Poland, Austria, much of the Germanies, and even France. And, while Russia was making substantial strides in the eighteenth century, Poland, Turkey, Italy, Austria, and Spain were actually regressing. It would be just as confusing to speak of the "industrial backwardness" of Russia in this era. In relation to whom? Industry was developing only slowly even in Britain, and Muscovite industrial development was surely the equal and more of most other parts of Europe. We are likely to learn far more, therefore, if we set aside the notion that Russia was qualitatively different from some unity called "Europe" or "the West," and if we deposit terms such as "underdeveloped" where they belong—in the post-industrial revolution.

Peter was a ruler vitally interested in the conditions of industry and commerce, more so than many of his illustrious European colleagues. His own common sense, added to his observations of the Dutch and the English in the Foreign Quarter and on the Grand Embassy, had convinced him that national economic prosperity and state strength were inextricably intertwined. He would have agreed firmly with the contemporary opinion of Ivan Pososhkov, the merchant-economist of his reign, that "in a Tsardom where people are rich, the Tsardom is rich, and in a Tsardom where people are poor, the Tsardom cannot be rich." Some historians have, therefore, insisted that Peter was a "mercantilist," and that this body of European economic doctrine stimulated Peter to widen his consideration of the Muscovite economy from largely a question of state income to that of the general prosperity of the nation. It is true that Baron Luberas, the Austrian collegial expert imported by the Tsar, did provide a memorandum which summarized many of the practices usually understood under the title "mercantilist": the dangers of exporting raw materials and importing manufactured goods, the dangers of state monopolization of commerce, the vast possibilities of Muscovite natural resources for the development of home industries, the advantages of resident Russian commercial consuls abroad, and the need for a College of Manufacturing to spur the economy. But it is also true that Baron Luberas did not enter Muscovy until 1717, and that Peter had already undertaken many of these economic programs and substantially set the direction of his policies.

On the other side of the argument, the distinguished historian B. H. Sumner called mercantilism "an epithet of mystifying vagueness," and Professor M. S. Anderson thinks it "increasingly doubtful that this term is a very useful one." [1] Peter wished to acquire hard currency, favored exports over imports, and instituted protective tariffs to stimulate home industries; but what aspiring monarch in Europe did not pursue these interests? Peter was no student of "western" economic theory, of which there truly was very little, but rather a student of Muscovite needs and of the Muscovite past. Peter was directed by no dogmas, but, as were most of his fellow princes, by his duties, by his inheritance, and by his ambition.

[1] B. H. Sumner, *Peter the Great and the Emergence of Russia* (New York: Collier Books, 1962), p. 144; M. S. Anderson, *Europe in the Eighteenth Century 1713–1783* (New York: Holt, Rinehart & Winston, Inc., 1961), p. 74.

More important to Peter than any theories of economic development abstracted from the empirical methods of the great Colbert were some Muscovite facts of life. The industrial and commercial enterprises of Muscovy were simply not prepared to handle the new demands of the Petrine state. A vast new market was created by the more sophisticated wars of the seventeenth century: the army required weapons, uniforms, equipment, and supplies, and the navy put special demands on a society totally unprepared for shipbuilding. At the same time the nobility was generating new demands for products and services. The general rise in population, a European phenomenon, also served to enlarge the domestic market. In most of the above, of course, the state was the overwhelming consumer.

Second, Peter inherited a domain in which economic development was not only ignored but actively resisted. Only the state was in a position to break down the more serious obstacles posed by Muscovite society, and Peter was well aware of this fact. His educational introduction to an enforcement decree could easily have been penned by an "enlightened" despot of the next century: "Because our people are like children about their learning, they will not learn the alphabet until they are forced by their master; at first they complain, but when they learn then they are thankful. . . . In manufacturing we apply not only proposals, but we also force and instruct and use machines and other measures to teach you how to be a good economist." Over and above social resistance, Peter also suspected the vast natural resources lying untouched in his domains and felt that only the state could force and could afford their exploitation.

Third, Peter lived with his own firmly forged political inheritance and his own political ambitions. An English traveler of the seventeenth century said of the Tsar Alexei that "he is the first merchant of his country . . . and the first manufacturer." One might go to the distant days of Kievan Rus to document the paramount role of the Russian prince in the economic life of his people, a role more central than that played by many western European counterparts. That heritage of state control, firmed in the tough wars of the seventeenth century, certainly limited Peter's options and certainly provided him with the kind of "modern" role which his contemporary monarchs had to struggle so hard to obtain. He was in no position and no disposition to surrender that role. Thus, Petrine involvement in economic development owed less to European theories than to the Muscovite past, the Muscovite present, and the absolutist aspirations of the Tsar. Peter was not so much the student of state-directed economies as he was one of the great formulators of this "modern" form.

Industrial and commercial development in eighteenth-century Russia, in the general European pattern, made no radical breaks with the preceding century. Muscovite industry of the seventeenth century was concentrated in mining and metals, in a small textile development, and in leather, paper, glass, and furs. The few large enterprises were owned by the state and the smaller private enterprises required special state assistance. Foreign commerce was firmly in the hands of the English and the Dutch, operating through the White Sea, while domestic commerce, limited and local, was supplied by native handicraft production.

It was vital for Peter to understand the serious obstacles faced by commercial and industrial enterprises in the preceding century. They struggled against overwhelming competition from cottage (or *kustar*) industries, from foreign companies, and from privileged groups. Nascent industry, as in the rest of Europe, competed much too unfavorably with cottage industries in the production of consumer goods for the domestic market. Also as in the rest of Europe, manufacturers paid a great deal of attention to production but very little to distribution, and thus, lacking even primitive means of transportation, could not compete in price or availability with peasant craftsmen in the villages. Muscovite industry and commerce also competed poorly with foreign goods which were cheaper, of better quality, and, a virtue which neither price nor quality could combat, more fashionable. Worse still, foreign companies made it a most successful practice to bribe their way into Muscovite markets. At the same time there were groups in the society, so-called "white" or privileged groups in the Church and the nobility, who manufactured and traded, but paid no taxes. To this triple competition must be added a lack of capital, an absence of technical skill, and the unpleasant reputation of Muscovite merchants; the propensity of these merchants to lie, steal, cheat, and connive was already a European watchword.

Petrine economic legislation was intended to remedy many of these problems. The sending of students abroad to acquire technical competence, while attractive to textbook writers, seems to have had no appreciable effect on economic development; indeed it produced negative effects in a "brain drain" and a "ruble drain" once the grand tour infected the aristocratic bloodstream. The importation of craftsmen was a bit more significant; Tsars Boris, Michael, and Alexei had set the style, and Peter made it a consistent policy after the first Azov campaign. Russian consuls abroad, growing in numbers, were assigned the task of enrolling such craftsmen for Russian service, and Peter himself had served as a recruiter on the Grand Embassy. The edict of 1702 circulated throughout Europe was designed "to encourage foreigners who are able to assist us in this way, as well as artists and artisans profitable to the state, to come in numbers to our country. . . .

There are several aspects to be noted about this importation of foreign craftsmen. First, these men were almost invariably in technical areas, especially shipbuilding, rather than in business organization. Second, while the number of these foreigners was great, it is also true that the bulk of the master smiths and carpenters and coopers were still Russians ordered into factory service. The foreigners who did accept service in Muscovy were often poorly treated and many complained bitterly that the agreements they had made with the Tsar were ignored. Lastly, in the interests of a fair perspective, one would do well to remember that Muscovy was not the only European state which made a practice of utilizing Dutch, English, and French craftsmen in their service: Austria, Sweden, Spain, and many others pursued similar policies.

Peter was also responsible for an enterprising survey of mining resources, originally undertaken in the hectic days after the defeat at Narva but refined and enlarged in the years after Poltava. The original Department of Mines was founded in 1700 and the College of Mines in 1719, with the Tsar's assurance that "our Russian land, more than any other lands, abounds in useful metals and minerals." Peat, coal, and oil surveys of the Voronezh region and of the valley of the Dnieper were undertaken, and comprehensive edicts issued for the preservation of forest resources. There was an attempt, largely successful, to introduce agricultural products which would provide raw materials for infant industries: flax, jute, hemp, tobacco, and even sheep.

Vital to the Tsar's program was the founding of companies under government order and direction. This was the policy after 1711, when the state's war initiatives were considered to require the involvement of private interests to insure their permanence. Tsar Peter was not entirely satisfied with the Muscovite institutions he had inherited. He would not work for the development of the *artels*, voluntary groups of artisans and craftsmen in the domestic market, because he considered them incapable of handling international business. Nor did he consider the seventeenth-century industrial association, a family unit under the direction of its elder, such as the Stroganov enterprise, to be a satisfactory vehicle. And so, beginning in 1700 but accelerating after 1711, Peter directed merchants and manufacturers to form companies as in other countries and to organize business councils to encourage economic development. As a matter of fact, Peter was ahead of many European princes in this regard: Austria's Ostend Company was not founded until 1722 and Sweden's East India Company even later. The English and the Dutch were much exercised by Peter's orders, feeling that the introduction of these companies might end their own exploitation of the Russian market and bring the Russians rapidly to control of their own economy.

To encourage his subjects to follow his orders and found companies, Peter legislated a series of incentives. State industries were to be handed into private control, as the Tsar instructed that "these manufactories and factories which have been, and those which will be, established by our treasury . . . shall be brought into good condition and be given out to private persons, and the College of Manufacture shall be responsible for them." The state monopolies in certain commodities were also to be given out to private commercial groups. Financial subsidies to new companies were provided, even at times when the war seemed to absorb all resources; liberal tax exemptions were provided, loans were extended without interest, and immunity from import taxes was granted for machinery, equipment, and materials. At the same time, the Tsar promised freedom from compulsory state service, civil or military, to owners, managers, their children, and skilled craftsmen of the new enterprises. The state was also instrumental, as we shall see, in providing a labor supply. Finally, the Tsar established protectionist tariff rates to encourage his budding companies.

The industrial enterprises which began to appear and spread in Peter's reign did not really indicate a substantial break with the seventeenth-century experience. Some of these industrial concerns were large for their day, employing from 700 to 1,000 workers, but even these were not yet unified "factories" in the sense that this word would be understood today; production was carried on in a group of scattered workshops or in the cramped huts of a village. These were "industrial settlements" rather than factories. State concerns were the largest; the Moscow Sail Cloth Factory had about 1,100 employees, the Sestrosersk Ironworks about 700, and the developing state-owned and private smelters and foundries in Perm Province had over 20,000 peasants attached to them. These Muscovite establishments were comparable in size and practice to the larger units in western Europe. And, contrary to usual expectations, the ownership and management of these newly sponsored industries were largely in Russian hands.

Nor was Petrine industry simply a war system or permanently under state ownership. Industrial development fell within the same divisions as other aspects of the reign. Before Poltava about 75 per cent of industrial enterprises which were founded were owned by the state and reflected military requirements, especially armaments, uniform cloth, and sailcloth. After Poltava, however, attempts were made to alter both the ownership and the direction of industrial growth. Silk, velvet, china, bricks, and other "consumer" products were encouraged, and many such factories were transferred into private hands. Only the forests and forest products remained under strong state management. It was still the duty of the College of Manufacture, however, to receive reports from industries, to assist them in difficult times, to receive samples of their work, "so that the College can see the quality of what they produce," and, in general, "to have direction like a mother over her children."

On the question of capital, all historians are agreed on at least one point: foreign capital was not available to support Muscovite industrial expansion in the Petrine period. Early Soviet historians made claims for the role of the Muscovite merchant class in accumulating capital so that they might posit "a commercial-capitalist stage" at the end of the seventeenth century. Other historians have disagreed, noting that most merchants were in rather poor condition and were themselves in constant need of government assistance. We can now see that the shortage of capital was a general European condition. The central role of the state in underwriting industrial expansion is demonstrated in the financial programs of the Muscovite government and in the practices of the College of Manufacture, which provided close supervision and substantial financial assistance even after many factories had passed officially into private hands.

Another key concern was labor; what was in a few western European states a natural process of change was in Muscovy a serious state problem. Muscovy, as did some other European states, had a class structure so solidified that no substantial group was being liberated from old strictures by historical forces to make it available for new uses. The Code of 1649, at the same time as it set the legal terms of Russian serfdom, also unconsciously set the defense for landed peasants against the harsh evictions and forced emigrations so common in nascent industrialism. Once again, only the state could crack this structure of law and custom, and once again the state's options were limited. Industrial workers had of necessity to be drawn from the serfs; historical debates as to the percentage of hired labor in Petrine industries do not change this fact. A decree of 1721 regularized the Petrine practice of granting to "merchants" who owned or managed enterprises the right to buy serfs "in order to increase the number of such mills" on condition that the serf village be forever attached to the enterprise and never sold apart. These "possessional" factories usually moved industrial techniques into the villages they purchased. Not only were owners entitled to buy serf villages from the nobility, but the government often staffed its own units and cooperated with private industries by assigning or ascribing state peasants to such enterprises. Such "ascribed" peasants were doubly unhappy, for they lost not only the guarantee of tenure on the land and were moved for "temporary" duty many hundreds of miles from home, but lost also the rather better status of the state peasantry. A decree of 1722 denied to landlords the right of recovery over serfs in factories. At the same time, the economic activism of the state common to this age struck the lowest elements in society in much the same way all across Europe; the days of the vagabond were at an end. The "poor laws" of western Europe were paralleled in Muscovy by Peter's conscription into industrial labor of orphans, women under sentence of crime, vagrants, and beggars.

The state also attempted to stimulate handicraft industries in the towns. Guild formation was decreed in 1722, with all craftsmen and even serfs with permits from their owners instructed to enroll themselves in such guilds. Masters were encouraged to enlarge the numbers of their apprentices and journeymen. The guild system, dying a struggling death in most parts of western Europe, did little to stimulate handicraft industries, which remained lodged in the peasant huts, even though the merchant Ivan Pososhkov in his book *On Poverty and Wealth* had been confident that "should craftsmen be prohibited from working as they please without supervision or civil administration, then all good artisans would enrich themselves and be as renowned as foreigners. Foreigners are no better than we, but have a strict civil code and are good masters; if we establish such a code, our craftsmen can surpass them."

The effects of this industrial legislation were several. First, industrial statistics were badly disarranged by "paper factories," by the practice of many individuals who registered as "manufacturers" in order to take advantage of the easy means of acquiring lands and serfs. Second, Petrine legislation created a group of factory owners and managers which enjoyed privileges surpassing even those of the nobility: freedom from state service, the right to own serfs, the right to harbor runaway serfs, and access to liberal government assistance. Finally, of course, the industrial system produced discontent; one need not be a Marxist to admit that industrial life in its infancy was a living hell for the workers in any part of Europe. Peasants, whatever the modern disposition to patronize them as miserable and backward, had an attachment to the land which was real for all their misery. The Petrine system tore them from that land, wresting from them the last meager benefit of serfdom, which was tenure on the soil. Iron discipline was maintained in state and private industrial enterprises, enforced by fines, beatings, and confinement in chains. Pososhkov spoke in extreme understatement when he criticized Russian factory managers who "do not value the worth of the Russian individual and do not wish to feed him sufficiently so that he will be content and without fear." Serfs so involved were little better than slaves, and the treatment of these industrial workers was a real factor in the peasant uprisings of the eighteenth century; the serfs of the Ural mines and foundries were prominent among the supporters of the Pugachev rebellion in 1774.

A special word must be said of the iron industry, for it was here that Russia performed most ably in the eighteenth century and here that the inappropriateness of the term "underdeveloped" for the Petrine economy is best seen. The Great Northern War had cut off the importation of iron from Sweden and of weapons from other states, and Peter was forced to enlarge native production to fill the gap. Four mining and foundry centers were active in Petrine Russia: Tula, Olonetz, Saint Petersburg, and the Urals. The first two had been active in the days of Tsar Alexei but had fallen off in production. Tula was reactivated by Peter and became the armament center for the whole Muscovite army. Smelting works were also reinvigorated at Olonetz on Lake Onega, expanding rapidly into a new Petrine city, Petrozavodsk, and in the area around Petersburg. In all cases water power resources were crucial, and Peter himself became a dedicated student of water mills. But the new symbol of Muscovy's industrial growth was Perm Province in the Urals, with its capital Ekaterinburg (named after Peter's second wife) on the Isset. Responsibility for most of these works was in the hands of the peasant Nikita Demidov, who was himself ennobled and sired a great industrial family. By 1725 there were nine state copper and iron works and twelve private works in operation in Perm province, producing in excess of 105,000 tons of pig iron and 3,200 tons of copper.

Peter left behind him some 200 large industrial enterprises, the major divisions of which represent the concentrations of Muscovite industrial growth: 69 in metallurgy, 23 in lumber, 17 in gunpowder, 15 in textiles, 14 in leather, 10 in glass, 9 in silk, 8 in sailcloth, and 6 in paper. The smelters and the foundries were the most successful, rising from 17 in 1695 to 69 by 1725. Pig iron production, which was one-fifth that of England in 1700, exceeded English production by 1725, Swedish production by 1775, and that of all Europe by 1785. Other industries were also making progress; textile production very nearly fulfilled Peter's injunction of 1712 that "textile mills will be increased throughout the country so that in five years it will not be necessary to purchase uniforms abroad." The leather industry was producing products well received in the rest of Europe. The original glass factory at Moscow, handed over to the management of William Leid of England in 1709, underwent a similarly rapid and successful expansion.

There were less fortunate aspects to industrial development. Government interference was the inevitable accompaniment and consequence of the state's central role as stimulater and consumer. The most efficient governments have been prone to high levels of interference in business, and one can only sympathize with the factory managers of Petrine Russia, who had at one and the same time to cope with the dynamic hopscotching of Peter and the ignorant tinkering of his ill-trained bureaucrats. One example might suffice: a government decree of 1715 ordered government purchase of bolts of cloth of a measurement which considerably exceeded the width of the old bolts; thus industry had to provide new looms, most of which could not be fitted into the huts where production took place. At the same time, in fairness to Peter, it must be admitted that his government's interference in business was far less extensive than that ascribed to Colbert in France. Even more serious than harassment by decree, entrepreneurs in Muscovy lived under constant threat of punishment for failure; the serious punishments meted out to those in the leather industry who were slow to adopt new oil-processing methods were paralleled in many other industries. This fear of government reprisals tended to throttle initiative and encouraged deceptive practices and reports.

Equally unfortunate for industrial development was the unwillingness of private capital, where it was accumulated, to put itself in jeopardy. The depreciation of the currency, the power of Peter's favorites to interfere and to embezzle, the absence of even rudimentary justice, all drove private resources elsewhere. Peasants, as peasants anywhere under such conditions, buried their rubles beneath the floorboards of their huts. Pososhkov, the merchant-observer of the Petrine economy, noted that "we will never attain renown while unhealthy judgements and uncontrolled administration cause damage and insecurity. . . . Judges see that the powerful and the liars attack others without cause but dare not interfere." In addition one can only wonder what progress would have been made in industrial development had not Peter been so prodigal with men and material; recall the vast investment of both in the Azov campaign before 1700, an investment completely liquidated thereafter. Finally one must note that it was not Peter's fault if after 1725 factories in several areas, such as silk, paper, and glass, were closed down for lack of competent management, unable to compete with favored foreigners and suffering neglect from the very government which had given them life.

Peter brought even more dynamism and interest to his policies for Russian commerce, for commerce was the preeminent pursuit of the age. The merchant Pososhkov assured the Tsar that "a Tsardom grows rich through its merchants, and without them not even the smallest state can survive." For the Tsar the patronage of a Russian merchantry was a domestic and a foreign matter. Peter saw the need to expand and enrich the merchant class both for its contribution to taxation and for its future role in industrial financing, which is a partial explanation for the system of self-government prescribed for towns as early as 1699. Peter saw also more clearly than many of his contemporaries that the destiny of the Russian merchantry was bound up with the international struggle for commerce. The Tsar would have agreed with the Englishman at the other end of the eighteenth century, quoted by Professor M. S. Anderson, who noted that "almost every corner of Europe, in our age, strives to gain some part of the commercial advantages which they clearly observe to contribute so much to the enrichment and exaltation of nations." [2] This is a partial explanation of the Petrine wars, as it was for most of the conflicts of the early modern era.

Peter was intent upon expanding the commercial groups in Muscovy and freeing them from restraints. The Code of 1649 had established townsmen with sole trading rights but, as noted earlier, privileged groups in the church and nobility, and even peasants in the rural villages had made this provision a dead letter. Peter had been considering these conditions even before 1700, but only after the crises of Poltava and the Pruth had passed did he act forcefully. In 1711 the Tsar ordered all these formerly privileged or illegally trading groups to commerce freely in his domains and to pay the taxes owed by all merchants. All distinctions and privileges were removed "so that all ranks of people may trade in any product anywhere under their own names, with payment of all customary taxes." Peasants were encouraged to register in towns for commercial affairs, an encouragement which varied directly with the amount of capital they had available. Thus, the tax rolls were to be enlarged, the commercial class widened, and unfair competition reduced. In 1719 Peter followed the direction of industrial policy and released many state trading monopolies in such products as furs, caviar, bristles, potash, pitch, rope, and leather goods to private interests. Actually, Peter in a few cases granted private trading monopolies, a practice which grew to disastrous proportions under his successors.

Peter also followed the lead of Vasili Golitsin and proceeded to establish permanent commercial representatives in other parts of Europe and in China. Consuls were appointed in Paris in 1715, in Vienna in 1716, in Peking and Cadiz in 1719, and in Liège and Bordeaux in 1723. Peter hoped especially to encourage direct commerce between France and Spain on one side and Muscovy on the other in order to break the lucrative hold of the Dutch and British on the carrying trade between southern Europe and the Baltic. Such plans, largely because of southern European indifference, were not successful.

Tsar Peter did not seriously alter the usual Muscovite tariff policies,

[2] Anderson, *op. cit.*, p. 54.

but he did extend, refine, and enforce them. Seventeenth-century tariffs were scaled less according to the value of the goods involved than according to the nationality of the shipper. This remained the pattern until 1724, with foreigners paying duties far higher than native shippers in the vague expectation that natives would thus be encouraged to take control of their own commerce. The impact of this approach was, of course, just the opposite: with their usual resourcefulness the Dutch and the English hired themselves Russian agents or "fronts" who shipped under a Russian name to take advantage of the beneficial tariff rates. Not only did this practice discourage development of native companies but it provided Peter and historians with a rather distorted picture of Russian commerical activity.

The Tariff of 1724 was a protectionist tariff which, while moving to rates based on kind and quality of goods and especially related to domestic production, still had the effect of discriminating by nationality. The highest customs rates, for example, between 50 per cent and 75 per cent *ad valorem,* applied to linens, silks, fine wines, furniture, and clothes which came almost exclusively from France, while the rates on English woolens were about 25 per cent. The tariff also tried to prevent the export of raw materials required for the development of native industries, such as hides for the leather industry, and flax and hemp yarns. This emphasis on protectionism must be conditioned, however, since it was selective and partial; Peter answered every request from state and private interests for total protection from foreign competition with the reminder that such protection would only be afforded when native production was fully supplying the domestic market.

The most startling development in Peter's commercial policy was the emergence of the new Baltic trade. The Great Northern War had brought into Peter's domain five thriving Baltic ports of venerable reputation: Riga, Pernov, Reval, Narva, and Vibourg. To these Peter had added the new city of Saint Petersburg and its naval base at Kronstadt, whose claim to the Baltic trade at its birth in 1703 was none at all. It was Peter's purpose to transfer the ancient White Sea trade of Archangel to Saint Petersburg in order to solidify the establishment of his new city by providing it with commercial as well as political and military foundations.

The diversion of the White Sea trade of Archangel to the Baltic port of Petersburg was no easy task. First of all, Dutch and the

English merchants resisted the change; they feared that the new port signaled the end of their exclusive control of Muscovite commerce and would encourage Russian carrying companies as well as introduce new competition from the German Baltic ports. Neither did the Russian merchants wish to support the change, and not for reasons of political reaction alone. The Dvina route northward to Archangel had been developed since the sixteenth century and was well traveled and well provisioned, while a route from the central provinces to Petersburg was nonexistent. Hardly encouraging to commerce were the remnants of roads which sank rapidly into the swamps, a barren land with no inns or stopping places, and a miasmatic, half-finished camp at the end of the journey. The costs of transport along these dismal routes greatly exceeded those of Archangel. Finally, both foreign and Muscovite merchants protested the excessive cost of life in Petersburg. Since there were no private residences or offices available in the city, they had to be built at extravagant cost with materials shipped overland from the central provinces. Even food had to be imported at prices two to three times normal in order to sustain life in this Baltic "paradise." If the reader can envision a frontier outpost, located in inaccessible northern lands where the winter clung till May, its scattered buildings sunken in mud, he can perhaps then better appreciate the reluctance of Muscovite and foreign merchants to risk their profits, their families, and their health to satisfy the whim of a fanatic Tsar.

Peter listened to none of the complaints and admitted none of the obstacles. It was an exercise fully worthy of the autocratic reformer at work. Those wealthy merchants whose business was heavily dependent on government purchases were simply ordered to transfer their offices and to build their homes in Saint Petersburg or lose their contracts. Reduced loading charges were mandated for Petersburg, and the Tsar designated certain key products to be shipped exclusively from his city. Peter gave much attention also to the luring of foreign ships to Petersburg, issuing special privileges to the first ships who would utilize the port. News of these grants sped rapidly along the Baltic, and the first Dutch ship entering Kronstadt was greeted in the overwhelming Petrine manner by the Tsar himself.

The most serious obstacle to Peter's plans for Petersburg was internal transportation. Peter initially undertook a series of roads in the north, but the work failed. The Moscow-Saint Petersburg road was a representative disaster, since the shortest route traversed the swamps and invariably sank in short order. Other routes were equally as dangerous and certainly more expensive. These failures led Peter back to his inheritance, the river routes of Russia, for a solution. Peter and his peasant advisor Serdhukov made a personal inspection of canal routes from Moscow to Petersburg past Tver and Novgorod. Peter envisioned a canal system ultimately of vast proportions linking a great quadrangle of Black, Baltic, White, and Caspian seas with the central provinces. Prince Menshikov was first placed in charge of the canal projects but, performing in his usual self-serving manner, was replaced in 1718 by a German engineer, General Munnich. Only one of the six projects came near completion in Peter's lifetime, and the most visionary awaited the Soviet period for achievement. The Baltic and the Caspian were linked in 1708 and reopened in 1732, but the route did not stay in repair for the rest of the century. Peter was well ahead of most of Europe, saving France, in his vision of canal transport in an age when improvement in land transportation was in no way comparable to the vast expansion of ocean routes.

Even with the momentous obstacles to be overcome, Peter's plan to replace Archangel with his beloved Petersburg was accomplished. Between 1700 and 1718 once thriving Archangel saw its commerce fall from 3 million to 300,000 rubles, while Petersburg's mounted in the same period from nothing to 4 million rubles a year. Ships annually frequenting the White Sea port fell from 126 to less than 50, while Petersburg rose from one ship in 1713 to 242 in 1725, with an additional 176 arriving at Narva. By the end of the eighteenth century more than three-quarters of Russian trade passed by Petersburg and Riga, with Petersburg commanding one half. It had been argued that Petersburg would have achieved this position naturally, if over a longer period, without all the violence and compulsion which only served to hasten the inevitable. These arguments, sensible as far as they go, fail to take into account that the existence of Petersburg was a political as well as an economic question, and that the city might not have existed at all at the end of the century had not Peter been so substantially successful in linking its political fate to the fate of Russian commerce. But more of that later.

All of this emphasis on Baltic commerce tends to obscure the development of Muscovite trade with the east. Much as it pleases us to tie Muscovy by bonds of business to the "west," it is still true that Turkey, Persia, the central Asian khanates, and China played important roles as well. Witness enough were Peter's Persian War in 1722, the treaties of Nerchinsk and subsequent agreements with the Chinese, the planning of the Bering expeditions to Kamchatka, and even visions of an Arctic sea route to Japan and beyond. Fyodor Saltykov, a Petrine advisor, told the Tsar that he "would be able to enter the East India trade, which would produce many benefits and great wealth, especially since your state is closer to that trade area than any other country." Muscovy was already emerging as an intermediary between eastern and western commerce, especially in the silk trade with Persia. It behooves those who speak of underdeveloped Muscovy to remember that this state under Peter was as much a colonizing and expanding empire as any of its "western" brethren. There is nothing in the definition of imperialism which requires its practitioners to cross any salty seas, and when the characteristics of early modern Europe are listed to include imperial expansion, Russia qualified with the rest.

Peter's commercial policy was, by the standards of his day, a grand success. The Tsar was the envy of his follow monarchs, for his accounts revealed a balance of exports over imports in 1725 to the extent of 2.4 million rubles to 1.6 million rubles, leaving him a delicious balance of payments. Russia was one of the very few countries with whom England's trade was continuously unfavorable, thanks to the export of naval stores and pig iron. There were, however, even by contemporary standards, major areas of difficulty in banking, organization, and the merchant marine. Of Russian banking in Peter's reign there is little to say; its foundations date from the reign of his daughter Elizabeth and even then they were primarily agricultural in focus. Peter failed to create a Russian merchant marine, and the Dutch and English maintained their hold on the carrying trade. Nor did the Russians really succeed in establishing any companies significant enough to take full advantage of the valuable exports of iron and naval stores. The statistics of his own day may even have served to delude or console the Tsar. Russian prejudice against goods shipped in foreign bottoms, for example, was circumvented by considering as Russian flag ships all those vessels whose crews were at least 10 per cent Russian. The profits of this paper merchant marine went to London, Amsterdam, Lübeck, or Bremen. And then there was the old question of Russians and the sea; for those enamored of theories of national characteristics there has always seemed ample evidence that Muscovites were ill-suited to sailing. It was certainly true in Peter's day that sea service was detested by aristocrat and peasant alike, but that was more common than not in at least half the states of Europe. It would indeed take time for Peter's inoculation to take effect and for the Russians to make themselves at home on the world's oceans, but at home they certainly have made themselves by the second half of the twentieth century.

Peter could not handle all the aspects of economic development of his realm in one lifetime; the adaptation of his citizenry to changing forms of economic life required more time than any human could hope to wrest from history. Even more difficult to posit in one generation were institutional foundations in banking, insurance, business organization, and technical training; the absence of a university tradition and a strong scientific heritage, for example, could hardly, as we shall see, be remedied by Peter before his reign's end. Which is to say that across the spectrum of European societies, the strongly traditional environments into which new state economic initiatives were thrust differed markedly and consequently produced a variety of responses with varying degrees of success. If one mentioned only a few elements of the Russian environment—the only recent acceleration of Muscovite secularization as compared with that of England or France, the overwhelming concern for defense against invaders and security from internal revolt which ran through the seventeenth century and well into Peter's reign, the rising rather than receding tides of serfdom—then we may better understand why the technical and educational foundations for an industrial leap based on the Petrine work were not as well prepared as in a few of the Atlantic seaboard states. We may understand also that the Petrine economic programs themselves may well have made necessary the continuation of a dominant state role to broaden and deepen the social foundations needed to insure the survival and growth of these programs.

It may still suit some political scientists to paint Peter as the first great opponent of Muscovite backwardness and some Soviets to find him a cozy niche in the dialectic as the tool responsible for "creation and strengthening of the national state of *pomeshchiks* and merchants." [3] But others might consider the struggles to fit Peter into twentieth-century economic formulations or into the dialectic to be badly misleading ones, and prefer rather to insert the Tsar once again into the eighteenth century. Peter's economic policy was that of an aspiring absolutist bureaucratic state, and contributed substantially

[3] Josef Stalin, quoted in P. I. Lyashchenko, *History of the National Economy of Russia to the 1917 Revolution* (New York, 1949), p. 267.

to the concepts of "enlightened despotism" of the next generation and many generations to come. Peter believed that the state should lay the foundations of national prosperity and conduct its subjects toward that prosperity. Every decree on economic matters contained an educational preamble which the Tsar considered as important as the compulsion being introduced, almost always written by the Tsar himself, which cajoled, reasoned, lectured, and explained the purposes of the legislation. Peter's espousal of the primary state role in ordering, disciplining, directing, and ultimately liberating the national economy for the general welfare is just as "western" and surely as "modern" an idea, for good or for evil, as free-enterprise capitalism or industrial socialism. And surely this modern idea owes far more to Peter than he owes to it.

☀ 7 ☀

The Church
and Secular Culture

The Church had been progressively losing sway in parts of Muscovite society throughout the seventeenth century. The emerging Romanov absolutism and its accompanying forces of secularization had challenged the place of the Church, and the Nikonian Schism had been a battle with these forces as well as a veritable civil war within the Church itself as to how best to carry on that battle. The effect of the Church's diminishing authority was to disorient and confuse the body of the faithful, who understood little of the forces at play or the issues at stake except that neither the Petrine government nor the Nikonian church seemed committed to the ancient spiritual values of Muscovy. And yet history abhors a vacuum; the void being left behind by the retreating Church was slowly being filled by secular forces, and the culture of Muscovy was fitfully reorganizing itself into "modern" form. It was precisely in those areas where the Church was losing its political and intellectual battles, on the levels of the state and the new service aristocracy, that it was being most rapidly displaced by secular culture; and it was precisely in those areas where the new state penetrated least, in the lives of the peasantry, that the spiritual forces maintained themselves in a confused state of defense. Peter's confrontation with the Church, then, was but the surface sign of a vast cultural transformation already under way in Muscovy.

But the secularization of culture was a European as well as a Muscovite phenomenon; it is one of those characteristics which we call "modern," meaning that it characterizes "western" culture since 1500. And lest we fall back again too heavily on the idea of "western" tutelage of Muscovy in this regard, let it be remembered that the battles of Church and secular forces were far from over in seventeenth- and eighteenth-century France, that Austrian secularization was really not in full flower until long after Peter, and that Spain's secularization may not yet be completed. The Church as a European institution was waging its most desperate battles for the hearts and minds of men, for control of educational systems, for preservation of its vast properties, for maintenance of its autonomy, both internally and against the newly rising monarchies in this age. Peter's struggle with his Church, then, was but the surface manifestation of a cultural transformation under way in all of Europe as well as in Muscovy.

There are those who have seen the physical symbols of the battle of secular and spiritual in the contrasting skylines of the two great Russian cities. Moscow's Kremlin is dominated by churches—the Annunciation, the Transfiguration, the Archangel Michael, Vasili the Blessed—and its suburbs are dotted with the remains of great monasteries. Saint Petersburg is dominated by state buildings—the Admiralty, the Peter and Paul Fortress, the Winter Palace—and its suburbs are dotted not with the humble houses of God but with the grandiose summer palaces of its rulers. It is a striking contrast, but one which must be held in restraint for the eighteenth century. Peter built the Nevsky Monastery in Petersburg as well as the buildings of state, and transferred the relics of the saint to his new city. Peter was still in his heart as in his title the Orthodox Tsar, as Louis XIV was still in his heart as well as his title His Most Christian Majesty. The institution of the Church may have been having the worst of it from the forces of absolutism and the new learning, but religion itself still had power to command the hearts of kings as well as commoners. Louis XIV was not Napoleon; Frederick William was not Hitler; Peter the Great was not Joseph Stalin; one can, in his zeal, paint the early modern age as a little too modern.

Peter's attitude toward the Orthodox Church was based on several substantial foundations. He was himself a devoted son of Orthodoxy, faithful to its doctrines, schooled in its ritual, and dedicated to its spread. But he had the same feeling towards its clergy as he had toward the *boyars* and the *streltsi:* that their ignorance and conservatism marked them as instruments of retardation rather than progress; his early anticlericalism had been revealed in his "All-Drunken Synod." Peter, although unconcerned with Church doctrine, considered the clergy to be his special agents for the moral education and advancement of the people, meaning, of course, that they should accustom the people to do the monarch's will. He found the Muscovite clergy to be serving just the opposite function: as the leadership of resistance to the new military and political reorganization. Peter foreshadowed his programs in an interview with the Patriarch Adrian in 1700: "The clergy are almost illiterate. They should learn to administer the sacrament before being ordained. To do this a teacher is needed—and not only one—and a definite place to teach in . . . and such a school would thus minister to civic life."

Peter was also suspicious of the political aspirations of Church leadership in Russia; he feared the role of such leadership in resisting his reforms and resented the claims of such leadership to rival his own authority. Peter claimed that the Patriarch aimed to become "a second sovereign possessing power equal to or above that of the autocrat." This was not just an expedient charge; Peter really believed it. The history of the Patriarchate had been a rather powerful one, despite the insistence of some historians to this very day in applying the term "caesaropapist" to it. The Patriarchate had been established in Muscovy as recently as the Time of Troubles, in 1589, and had really been functioning for only a century; it was hardly an ancient institution and did not conjure up the cloak of venerability historians have assigned to it. Yet, in the short period of its existence it had produced patriarchs whose claims to authority had easily challenged the Tsars. Patriarch Hermogen had been the symbol of national unity in the war of liberation culminating in 1613, when there was no tsar. Patriarch Philaret, father of Tsar Michael Romanov, had been the first choice of the assembly of 1613 for Tsar had he not been in a Polish prison, and was virtual ruler for his son after his return and consecration as Patriarch. Patriarch Nikon had made claims to equal status with the Tsar Alexei, and even shared the title "Great Sovereign" with him. So Peter had reason to ponder the influence of this relatively recent centralizing and absolutist church leadership. He had also, in the persons of Patriarchs Joakhim and Adrian (who were both intimates of his mother) reason to suspect the dedication of the Church leadership to his programs. Dogma had little to do with it; the tradition of Patriarchal power tied to Patriarchal resistance to his will were sufficient excuses for Peter's antipathy.

Peter also had an argument with the Church over its material resources. As with every European monarch of his age, he was extremely covetous of Church property. Nontaxable income, property, and serfs had been accumulated by the Church over the centuries, and that Church could not be allowed to stay "a state within a state" or to sequester these resources while the state stood in desperate need of them. This general European problem had produced a variety of responses, including the laws of *mortmain* in England and in France, the visitation of the monasteries in Tudor England, and the secularization of property in revolutionary France. Peter himself had some precedent in the reign of his father, when Tsar Alexei had attacked Church courts and independent incomes; Nikon complained bitterly that the state was making itself like to God and that, in words not far from those of Thomas à Becket, "the Lord's property and the Lord's courts are being transferred in the name of the Tsar."

Peter had reasons to wish the Church more amenable to his control, and he had Muscovite practice and European experience to direct his way. The Muscovite inheritance was vital, for when Peter launched his reform of the Church, in the words of the historian Paul Miliukov, "the front-line defenses already had been captured."[1] The Nikonian Schism had robbed the official Church of the devoted support of pious Muscovites, so that it was weakened from below. The same Nikonian reforms had driven many prelates and lower clergy into resistance, so that they fled to the Old Belief or were retired, and in every case Peter was quick to make his own replacements, usually with clergymen trained in Kiev, so that the official Church was infiltrated from above.

Peter had been growing more and more annoyed at the role of the Patriarch in crystallizing resistance to the changes the Tsar thought expedient. It will be recalled that the Patriarchs Joachim and Adrian were bound in Peter's mind to the benighted court of his late mother, and that the Patriarch Adrian had been consecrated in 1690 much against Peter's better judgment. Adrian hated foreigners and foreign ways, lectured the Tsar on the manner of his life, chided him for his travels abroad, roared against the social innovations of 1698–99, and condemned the Tsar's treatment of his wife and child. It was no surprise when, at Adrian's death in 1700, Peter postponed the appointment of a successor. Almost all historians agree that Peter did not at that time plan to strike down permanently the office of Patriarch, but that the necessary reorganization of the state in the wake of the battle of Narva would simply go more smoothly without a reactionary Patriarch to impede every step. The confiscation of the church bells of north Russia in order to cast emergency artillery pieces, for example,

[1] Paul Miliukov, *Outlines of Russian Culture, Part I: Religion and the Church* (New York: A. S. Barnes and Co., 1960), p. 130.

certainly would have called forth a condemnation from Adrian. Peter appointed one of his favorite clergymen, Stefan Yavorsky, as "Exarch, Guardian and Administrator of the Holy Patriarchal See," and in the midst of the national emergency diverted Church and monastery incomes to a government department. This arrangement lasted until the permanent reorganization of Church affairs in 1721.

The future disposition of what was in its origins a rather pragmatic Church reform was not directly in Peter's hands; he was far too busy with the war and its demands. The organizational form of Orthodoxy was actually debated between two intriguing prelates who lost no time in falling into a classic argument about the proper relationship between Church and State. One of these was Stefan Yavorsky, Guardian of the Patriarchal See, and the other was Feofan Prokopovich, Archbishop of Novgorod and, ultimately, the author of the Church reform of 1721. Their careers and their conflicts revealed much about Petrine Russia.

Stefan Yavorsky was born in 1658 and died before the Tsar in 1722. He began his career in the turbulent Ukraine of the seventeenth century at the celebrated Kievan Academy, and took a well-worn road to Roman Catholicism. It is startling to discover just how many of the Kievan clergy had flirted with Catholicism in the second half of the century, even to the point of temporary conversions. Yavorsky was himself a convert to Catholicism and a student of the Jesuits in Poland, who had then lapsed back into Orthodoxy. These lapsed Catholics were excellent teachers in the spirit of the Kievan Academy, for no one knew better than they the techniques of their Jesuit antagonists. Yavorsky met Peter in 1700 and it is said that the Tsar had never heard such learned and inspiring oratory from any of his backward clergy. The Tsar must indeed have been impressed, for Yavorsky was Metropolitan of Riazan and Keeper of the See before the year ended.

Yavorsky was of one mind with the Tsar in demanding an educated clergy, but as the years passed it became clear that he was not of one mind with the Tsar on the proper relationship between Church and State. Yavorsky was labelled a "papist" in his own day, and the accusation was not far wrong although "Nikonian" might have been more in the spirit of the times. If Yavorsky supported the Tsar's notion of a reformed and enlightened clergy, it was not for Peter's purposes of creating a moral police force for the state but for the Church's purpose of defending itself against subjugation by the state. Yavorsky did indeed admire the organization of the Church of Rome; it was in the Papacy that he found the strongest instrument for the preservation of church independence. Nor was it strange in an age which exalted absolutism all over Europe as a progressive principle most efficient for national development, that the benefits of such authority should have been similarly pursued to solve the problems of the beleaguered Church. Yavorsky favored a strong leader for Orthodoxy, to give it identity, to reawaken it in eastern Europe and in the Balkans, and he saw himself as the Patriarch who would consummate the Nikonian reforms and lead a great spiritual revival.

Yavorsky perhaps exemplified the dangers of enrolling bright young men with strong opinions in the service of the crown—they came equipped with their own visions. If a nobody was appointed, nothing would be done; if a whirlwind was appointed, who could foretell what would be done? Besides, Yavorsky was an honest man in a court of thieves. He could not stomach much of Peter's private life and, to give Peter his due, Yavorsky's career was testimony to the Tsar's tolerance of criticism high in the offices of state. Yavorsky denounced the secret police, defended the Tsarevich, and criticized Peter's second marriage. He was often forced to apologize and more often forbidden to deliver a sermon which he had planned. His influence on Church affairs naturally waned, but he continued to occupy his posts and to make his case for church government to the end. His constant pressure for the restoration of the Patriarchate may have helped cement Peter's decision to have none of it. Yavorsky, for instance, replied to an inquiry from the theologians of the Sorbonne concerning the reunification of churches: "As it is, the Russian Patriarchal See is vacant; and for the bishops here to ponder over any question in the absence of the Patriarch is similar to the limbs of a headless body wanting to move or the stars following their course without an initial impetus. These extreme circumstances are depriving us of speech and action." Yavorsky spoke for the "catholic" position on church and state, but there was little chance that the position that had already lost to the English and Spanish kings and was at that time being subjected to the Gallican Liberties of France would ever triumph in Russia after the failure of Nikon.

Yavorsky's talented opponent and ultimately his nemesis was Feofan Prokopovich, born in 1681 and active in Russian politics well after Peter's death. Prokopovich's early career was similar to that of

Yavorsky: education at the Kievan Academy, conversion, in his case, to the Uniate Church, several years of Catholic education at Rome, reconversion to Orthodoxy in 1702, and a professorship at the Kievan Academy. Peter encountered him on a visit to Kiev in 1706 and soon raised him to Director of the Kievan Academy. Prokopovich's keys to preferment were his sermons for great occasions, in the style of the great Bossuet; he celebrated the glorious victory of Poltava from his pulpit and lavished unstinting praise on Peter and his cohorts. His skill carried him into the Orthodox hierarchy and ultimately, in 1724, to the Archbishopric of Novgorod.

Prokopovich, student of Roman Catholicism, emerged from his experiences in Rome a dedicated opponent of its claims to authority. He was a Protestant sympathizer; as he labeled Yavorsky a "papist," Yavorsky in turn knew a "Calvinist" when he saw one. "Erastian" would have been a more accurate title, for Prokopovich inveighed against Church property and Church autonomy. He crystallized the Tsar's ideal of "a divinely guided police state," to use the felicitous phrase of Professor Michael Florinsky.[2] Aside from his ideological ties to Peter, Prokopovich did noble service as the Tsar's premier propagandist. Once again the parallel with Bossuet is striking. No government action was too filthy or too demeaning for Prokopovich to justify it or to decorate it with the lessons of the New and Old Testaments, even to the Tsar's execution of his own son. Prokopovich was equally as ambitious as Yavorsky, but not nearly so honest, and infinitely more in tune with the times. It was to him, therefore, that the creation of the Church reform, the Spiritual Regulation of 1721, was naturally entrusted.

The Spiritual Regulation eliminated the office of Patriarch of the Russian Orthodox Church. In its place was established the Holy Synod composed of eight members of the hierarchy, a collegial form of administration to match the other colleges such as Foreign Affairs and Commerce. Said the regulation: "From the collegial principle the state has no need to fear rebellion and disturbance such as arise from the spiritual regulation of a single individual, for whom the common people cannot distinguish spiritual power from the power of the autocrat . . . but think that he is a second sovereign with similar or greater powers. . . ." The theme of the Regulation was the theme of

[2] Michael T. Florinsky, *Russia: A History and an Interpretation* (New York: The Macmillan Company, 1953), Vol. I, p. 413.

state absolutism: that one power alone was required and that the people ought not to be confused by conflicting allegiances. The Church had become a department of the state.

The presiding officer of the Holy Synod was the Chief Procurator, and it was Peter's wish that the Procurator be a reliable military man. The office, from Peter's day until the end of the monarchy, was always in the hands of a layman close to the throne and a potent spokesman for the autocracy. The Holy Synod rapidly assumed control of Church income, clerical appointments, and Church building. All the clerical members of the Synod took an oath to "accept the Monarch of All Russia, Our Gracious Lord, to be the final judge of this college." Peter sent his agents to visit the bishops and abbots of the realm to secure their approval of the reform; it was a simple choice of sign or resign. They all signed.

A significant part of the Spiritual Regulation dealt with the problems of the education of the clergy. Such a reform might seem to a modern reader so sensible as to require no defense, but Prokopovich had to harness all his persuasive powers to convince the clergy that education was not some evil instrument bound to corrupt them: "Many foolishly assert that instruction is the cause of heresy. But heretics of ancient days raved not through instruction but through arrogant foolishness. . . . Good and useful instruction is the root and seed and foundation of all usefulness, both for the fatherland and the church." The Regulation prescribed the establishment of schools for every diocese and created a syllabus for priestly education which was quite liberal in its requirements. A certificate of education was required before priestly ordination could take place. More than forty seminaries were established as a result of the reform.

The Tsar's concern with monasteries and monks was by no means as solicitous as that displayed for the regular parish clergy. The parish clergy were instruments of the state for the moral education of the people and the justification of the Tsar's will, even utilizing compulsory confession of sins for all the faithful to gather information about crimes of state interest. But what functions did monks perform for the state and what value did they produce? The number of monks and nuns had mounted to 25,000 by the beginning of Peter's reign. Both the Tsar and Prokopovich were "protestant" enough or "mercantilist" enough or "pragmatist" enough to feel that daily prayer was hardly a useful state service meriting reward. "Our monks are too fat. The gates of heaven are faith, prayer, and fasting; I'll put them on the road to

Paradise with bread and water and not with sturgeon and good wine."
In 1723, Peter attacked the monasteries as subversive centers full of
"useless hands" and attributed their strength to the malignant influence of former Patriarchs: "This gangrene among us was spread
first under the protection of those Church Monarchs!" The Tsar issued
a decree forbidding any more enrollments in monastic orders without
his permission; henceforth the Tsar filled the monastery rolls at the
death of incumbents from the lists of needy military veterans. Monasteries could at least provide homes for old soldiers.

There are debates about Peter's Church reform. Some historians
hold that the reform was the most carefully organized and the most
radical of any of his programs because the destruction of the Patriarchate had no precedents in the Muscovite past. While it is surely true
that the Church reform was the most clearly organized by the best
minds over the longest period of time, that does not certify its radical
nature. The abolition of the Patriarchate was spectacular and called up
images of German princes and English kings repudiating the Roman
pope, but it is well to remember that the Patriarchate was a most
recent institution, that its career had been stormy, and that the
Spiritual Regulation spoke compellingly of a return to the ancient
methods of Church government. Even the other Patriarchs of the
Orthodox world, though they could hardly effectively resist, made no
objection to the acceptance of the Holy Synod as their "brother."

Another debate exists over the general effect of the Church reform.
Most historians have judged that the Church declined as an influence
in Russian life in the so-called Synodal Period, that as a department of
the state it stood lonely and miserable between two camps and enjoyed the allegiance of neither: the church was alienated from the
rapidly secularizing nobility on the one hand and from the popular
faith of the peasantry on the other. Its only mission was that of a
policeman enforcing the government's will. A slight disclaimer has
been registered to this prevailing view which holds that an educational, spiritual, and missionary revival followed the Church reform.
Even granting signs of vitality in the post-Petrine Church, the bulk
of evidence is still with the "classic" view.

Some observers have seen in Peter's Church reform merely the end
of the long drift to caesaropapism inherent in Byzantine tradition and
Muscovite practice. The Byzantine-Muscovite tradition was never
caesaropapist; if any theory was appropriate it was the Galatian
formula of the two swords of Church and State wielded over the world

in harmony, rendering unto Caesar what was Caesar's and unto God what was God's. But it may be true in history that caesaropapism and theocracy are the poles of the Church-State argument toward which the ideal mean bends to one side or the other. It was simply that by the end of the seventeenth century "modern" requirements and techniques all benefited Caesar rather than God and tipped the balance permanently in Caesar's direction.

It is easy to see the forces let loose on the side of the state: a new military caste, an ambitious bureaucracy, secular learning and accompanying philosophies of government, blossoming commerce and industry, and intrusive new cultural forms. But there were internal factors as well restricting the Church's ability to defend itself. The analysis of Professor Miliukov is intriguing here, for he places as much responsibility upon the Church for its fate as he does upon the absolutist state.[3] Roman Catholicism, and we might add Islam as well, had built into its system a technique for handling developing doctrine not enunciated or sharply defined by the Church fathers. The later "slavophiles" of nineteenth-century Russia launched the label "rationalist" against the Catholic Church, and rationalist it was in the sense that the papacy developed its duties as expositor and teacher of an unfolding faith which revealed itself in accord with the needs of each age. The role of such Church leadership was creative.

No such tradition developed in Orthodoxy, where Church leadership took as its duty not the exposition of unfolding doctrine but the static defense of the faith from attack and protection of the original truths from erosion. The work of the Orthodox hierarchy was less creative than administrative; the Patriarch was not an interpreter but, as Peter described the work of the Exarch, "the supreme defender . . . protector . . . and guardian of the doctrines of the faith." But if protection was the primary duty of Orthodox leadership, then it was clear by the end of the seventeenth century that the Tsar could protect the faith, hound out the heretics, and support the missionaries far more efficiently than could the Patriarch. Consequently, the Tsar was never obliged to deal with the dilemma of who was "head of the Church," since the Tsar performed no doctrinal or theological functions. Doctrine was enshrined and now need be but preserved from violation. It was not simply Peter's character which explained his lack of involvement with Church doctrine but the tradition of his Church as

[3] P. Miliukov, C. Seignobos, L. Eisenmann, *Histoire de Russie* (Paris: Ernest Leroux, 1932), I, 409–10.

well. It is easier to see, in this light, why the Church so feebly defended itself against Peter's reform. It had neither popular support, nor aristocratic allegiance, nor inward resources to sustain it into the modern age.

But Church hierarchies and institutions are not necessarily, in fact all too seldom, the repository of living faith. Faith was still in the Russian people, and substantial numbers of them failed to follow their leaders into the Synodal Period. The most obstreperous resistance to the Synodal Reform was naturally found among the followers of the Old Belief; for them the reform was another confirmation of the reign of Antichrist and they withdrew the more from the main stream of modern history. It will be important to discuss these Old Believers as part of the resistance to the Petrine reform; here let us consider them as representatives of the fate of popular faith.

Peter's early social reforms on his return from Europe in 1698, his attacks on beards and Muscovite clothing and the old calendar, had sufficed to prove to those in the Old Belief and many others besides that Christ had departed from the Tsar and his servants. Numerological calculations identified the year of the Apocalyptic Beast and forecast the destruction of the world in 1702. "The Liers in Coffins" and the "Hiders in Trees" were out in full force as the new year arrived, but they suffered the terrible confusion of those whose prophecies of the world's end do not materialize. They had awaited the abomination of desolation as spoken by the prophet and had lived through another winter day like many others. What to do now? Many simply recalculated and waited, but that was no solution as days of abomination came and went. The world continued, and those who maintained that Antichrist now reigned over it had to answer a basic question: was the Church still alive? Two basic responses were given by the Old Believers. The "Priestless" considered that Orthodoxy had fled the world and that God's people were without priests, sacraments, or solace. The "Priestists," on the other hand, considered that while Antichrist reigned in Petersburg the battle for the faith still raged and that God's communities had to be staffed and protected by priests of the Old Belief.

The Priestless, the abandoned people of God, were the most radical. If the world was fallen into evil days, then flight was the only recourse and resistance the only good act. Into the northern provinces and into Siberia they went, where priests were hard enough to find in any case. They gathered into communities, confessed to one another, performed their own marriages; they were frightened in a world where they seemed to be forsaken. Peter was willing to tolerate the incredible opinions of these radicals if they but paid and served. The best-developed of these Priestless communities had emerged on the River Vyg in the 1690's when Sophia and Natalia had both made it clear that they did not intend to roll back the Nikonian Church. Under the paternal care of Daniel Vikhulin and Andrew Denisov, the Vygorsk community began to make commercial contacts with similar communities on the borders of the realm, establishing a merchant tradition that became a vital force among the Old Believers.

The Priestists, the larger of the segments of the Old Belief, were essentially compromisers who tried to thread their way between the radical views of their Priestless colleagues and the equally radical demands of the satanic society which reigned in Petersburg. They formed their communities, sought out sympathetic priests and bishops, and strove to keep the ancient worship alive in the land. Peter's treatment tended to perpetuate both branches of the Old Belief, since he would tolerate those who paid the price. Taxes on the Old Believers were doubled in 1716 and seemed to have been paid. Old Believers among the merchantry tended also to inspire Peter with a toleration born of respect for their industry and their income. The same attitude prevailed among bureaucrats and industrial managers; the rather large migration of schismatics into the Urals provided such energetic workers and craftsmen that some government officials made only a pretense at enforcing persecutions.

It is frustrating to be almost completely without statistics on the numbers of those actively following the Old Belief in Peter's reign. Rather unreliable government statistics of the nineteenth century showed 8.2 million in 1863, while some historians think the number nearer 10 million. Whatever their numbers in Peter's time, they were extremely influential not only in defining the discontents of the age and in infiltrating the growing merchantry, but in inspiring the rest of the population. They appealed not only to those who shared their spiritual beliefs, but also to that much larger group who identified them with open resistance to the overbearing state. How many among the presumed pacific peasantry of Russia who did not flee to build their communities in uneasy parallel with the cities of the new Russia but stayed upon their lands, how many of these had their hearts with the Old Belief? They would surface on and off in the century, as in the contingents of the rebellious Pugachev. When one speaks of the basic spirituality of the Russian peasant, therefore, one had better be ready to make distinctions and to admit ignorance. As in most cases with reforms, Peter had not created the Old Belief but he had certainly accelerated its development and in the process had driven another wedge into the ever-widening gap between Muscovite and Imperial society.

The retirement of the Orthodox Church from its ancient role in Muscovite society and the confrontation between state absolutism and personal faith were followed and accelerated by the rising secular forces the state was releasing. Professor Marc Raeff says of the Church in the eighteenth century that "as an institution the Church had ceased to be a social and intellectual authority for the nobility of Russia (if it ever had been one), for its traditional precepts could hardly satisfy the needs of individuals living in an environment so utterly unlike that of Old Muscovy." [4] The Church could not continue as of old in Russian society, for its areas of strength were never primarily theological, but surface and social, reflected in the rituals of worship, the social customs, the dress, the habits, the manners of the people, their literature, and their schools. Yet it was in these areas of culture and society that the state reforms were making their impact, sometimes consciously and sometimes unconsciously, leaving the Church no significant role and no substantial refuge.

Peter's attacks on the social customs of Muscovy were therefore the most direct and the most resented of the reforms. Beginning in 1698, beards were subjected to heavy taxes, the manufacture of old-style garments was forbidden, and German and French styles were prescribed. In these cases the social changes were forced upon the aristocrats with effect, but peasants and parish clergy could avoid them if they stayed away from towns and cities. The reform of customs, then, simply served to dredge deeper the ditch between the people and their nobility.

The transfer of the capital to Saint Petersburg accelerated the creation of an upper class secular culture. In the city, foreign dress was combined with new styles in residence, new forms of entertainment in the theater and music, new forms of decoration and display, all secular and self-glorifying. Dwellers in the city were encouraged by the best-selling guide to manners, *The Honorable Youth's Mirror*, to reshape their behavior in a modern form: "Young men should always

[4] Marc Raeff, *Origins of the Russian Intelligentsia* (New York: Harcourt, Brace & World, Inc., 1966), p. 153.

employ foreign languages when conversing, in order to practice. This is especially so when they wish to discuss something confidential so that menials will not know of it, and also so that they will not be thought ignorant asses. . . ." Peter actually issued a decree forbidding lower clergy and peasants clad in the old style from entering his city lest visitors be shocked at their backwardness. Peter did not transform the culture of the Russian aristocracy as easily or as rapidly as he tied them to service, but he did addict them to new ways, introduce them to a cosmopolitan outlook, force them to confront other European forms of art and architecture, and compel them to become the premier tourists of Europe.

Symbolic of the enforcement of the new styles and customs upon at least the upper portion of his society were the Tsar's "social assemblies." The Decree on Assemblies of 1718 ordered nobles to come together to practice the social graces. "*Assemblée* is a French word, not expressable in any one Russian word; to explain its meaning, it is a free meeting in a house which encompasses both pleasure and business, where people can meet and converse about all manner of things and learn what is passing around them. . . ." These enforced social schools were held weekly in the homes of the court nobles, with men and women mingling together in direct violation of Muscovite custom. Peter also ordered that no one should use the old marks of respect when he appeared, and the punishment for such a lapse was consumption of a large glass of wine.

The literature of the age was similarly affected by the reforms. Petrine literature may not have been very significant in critical terms, but it was certainly revealing of the times. How symbolic that the eminent historian of Russian literature, D. S. Mirsky, should insist that "of the original writings of the period those of Peter himself are easily the best." [5] The works to which Mirsky refers are the Tsar's decrees, dynamic expressions of the will of the state for the new age. The bulk of Petrine literature was work in technical translation consisting of guides, handbooks, texts, and engineering manuals. It was ironic also that the best work of the Churchmen of the era should be most strongly represented by Feofan Prokopovich, whose sermons and plays radiated the glory of the state rather than the glory of God; his drama *Saint Vladimir* celebrated, in carefully drawn parallels with the work of Peter, the triumph of Vladimir of Kiev over the heathen priests, and

[5] D. S. Mirsky, *A History of Russian Literature From Its Beginnings to 1900* (New York: Vintage Books, 1958), p. 34.

his *Justice is the Monarch's Will* was the most substantial apology of the age for the new absolutism. And how galling to the clergy that the most popular book of the day was not a work of hagiography but a translation from German of a book of social etiquette. Symbolic, too, that the first Russian newspaper, *Vedomosti*, published in 1703, was devoted to war news rather than to religious homilies. The foundations of the study of Russian history were similarly laid, not to glorify the role of God's people but to justify the triumph of the state and to present a decent face to other states of Europe. Even the novels of this era circulating in manuscript took a Petrine theme and grafted it to the romantic adventure form of the seventeenth century: young noble traveling in western Europe encounters true love.

Even more revealing than the content of literature was the condition of the Russian language. Old Church Slavonic, the tool of the Church for transmitting the liturgy and the lives of the saints, was far from the oral language of the people and unequal to the task of conveying modern notions of war and administration. Church Slavonic had been undergoing changes in the seventeenth century, largely generated by the Kievan Academy, but its vocabulary was too limited and its atmosphere too antipathetic to handle the Petrine deluge of translations. A popular Russian language, full of Slavonic remnants and bloated by a deluge of foreignisms to modernize it, emerged as the necessary tool for the communication of ideas in the new age. The result was a crude hodgepodge which required the work of eighteenth-century grammarians to regularize. In 1708 the Tsar reformed the alphabet to make printing easier with what was symbolically called "the civic alphabet," and another blow was struck at the Church, whose works retained the old alphabet and promised to fall out of touch with the new generations. If nothing was produced to grace the literary history of Russia, a great deal had been done to enrich and to force the reshaping of the language which would one day make such productions possible.

Art and architecture revealed the same kind of peripheral effects of the Petrine reforms. Peter provided no real guidance to the arts, and their development was largely an afterthought to the main thrusts of the reign. Indeed, much of Peter's contribution was to remove serious obstacles to the development of movements which had emerged in the seventeenth century and to provide a receptive aristocratic stratum into which these new modes in art and architecture could be, in time, received and nurtured. In the seventeenth century, for example, state buildings in the new baroque style imported through Ukraine were more and more in competition with Church architecture. Even icon painting, so often portrayed as immutable in its preservation of sacred portrayals, underwent changes in the direction of realism; the works of Simon Ushakov were startling in this regard. Even portraiture was developing in the hands of German and Dutch painters in the Palace School despite the attacks of Patriarch Nikon. Perhaps the greatest contribution of Peter to the release of these forces was the building of Petersburg, for the city which epitomized the Petrine state had to be glorified. It was the last monumental opportunity of the eighteenth century for such extensive application of the arts. Imported architects, Trezzini, Schluter, Mattarnovi, LeBlond, all supported by minute regulations for building and decoration, established the plans for the glorious state buildings and private palaces which celebrated the new secular values: the College Buildings, the Summer Palace, The Kunstkammer, the Menshikov Palace, the Admiralty, and the Peter and Paul Fortress—each a monument to the new forces being released into Russian life.

The arts were patronized primarily for state purposes. Engravers were encouraged for their contributions to text illustration. Portraitists and sculptors were commissioned to produce what we might call "civic icons"; the Tsar ordered aristocrats to have their portraits painted or sculpted for their homes and public buildings in order to inspire respect in all their subjects. The elder Rastrelli did just such work for Menshikov and for the Tsar himself. Engraved prints were also circulated for the purposes of propaganda, exalting victories and encouraging civic virtue. It is a good example of the way in which state devices could be transformed rapidly into popular ones that prints began to appear that ridiculed the government. Particularly striking was the engraving of "The Cat," his face clearly identified as the Tsar Peter by the moustache which inspired the Old Believers to identify him with this animal, with the satiric caption: "He lives gloriously, eats agreeably, and farts gently." Similarly widespread was the cartoon of the happy mice burying a very Petrine looking cat.

Educational reforms were also an outgrowth of state needs. In this case the reforms were an intentional excursion of the Tsar into cultural life, but even if intentional they were not nearly as effective as those in war and administration. The gap between good intentions and practical fulfillment was widest in educational reform, largely because Peter was not as familiar with the problems of education as he was with those of the battlefield or the factory, nor did he ever take the time to so familiarize himself. To fight battles Peter had himself first learned to be a soldier, to establish factories he had first learned the crafts and skills, but to found schools he had himself never been willing to endure one.

At Peter's accession the only schools in Muscovy were those of the Church designed to train the clergy; they were usually attached to monasteries, bishops' residences, and parish churches. The best of these Church schools operated under the intellectual aegis of the Kievan Academy of the Ukraine, with its reflection in the Latin-Greek-Slavonic Academy in Moscow, but the bulk of the schools were poor and completely disparate in their curriculums and teaching levels. They were provided with no elementary school foundations, which were presumed to be the business of the family, and they were lacking in any secular disciplines. The Academies might reach several hundred laymen a year, but education for the rest of the population came only through the liturgy. Any advanced education for laymen was a matter of private tutoring. Even the printing of books was a traditional Church prerogative, which obviously limited the secular works available to literate Muscovites.

Peter, as usual with his reforms, began in the middle, discovered the necessary steps he had overlooked, and then went off in all directions to correct them. Petrine schools were born of the need for trained administrators and were aimed at providing a quick solution to the state's manpower needs. The Tsar had little patience with visions of intellectual enlightenment; his needs were practical, as he informed the Patriarch Adrian: "Well-learned persons are required by the state for all purposes. They can go into church service or the civil service or they can enter army service; they must know how to build and achieve the doctor's art of healing." Peter introduced technical schools, the first in Russian history, with the aim of staffing his civil and military services. The Greek-Slavonic Academy in Moscow was Latinized in 1701, enlarged with Ukrainian clergy, and ordered to broaden its curriculum. More innovative was the School of Mathematics and Navigation, founded the same year in the Sukharev Tower in Moscow and moved to Saint Petersburg in 1715 with other state agencies under the name of the Naval School. This school, planned on the English style, was directed by a Scot recruited during the Grand Embassy. Its courses were taught in English and its curriculum of arithmetic, geometry, geography, fortifications, mechanical drawing, and gunnery seemed more relevant to the new age than the classical studies still widespread in the rest of Europe. In the early years the school's three teachers did nothing but try to collect their back salaries, but it averaged about 300 pupils a year after the Tsar began to compel his nobles to attend. Thereafter came the Engineering School (1711), the Artillery School (1717), and the School of Surgery (1717), each averaging about 55 students annually, and other small mining schools in the Urals.

It was obvious from the early experiences of the Mathematics School that some sort of basic foundation was required before these upper schools could be effective. Learning to read and write, for example, might reasonably be considered a prerequisite to the study of geometry or the preparation of diplomatic correspondence or the keeping of state accounts. The attempt to provide this basic introduction for nobility, clergy, and even some of the middle class took two forms. The western missionary schools, such as Pastor Gluck's Lutheran Gymnasium, were unpopular and short-lived. The Mathematics Schools, popularly called "cipher schools," were decreed in 1714 for the mandatory education of the sons of the nobility, clergy, and middle class from ages ten to fifteen, and two graduates were to be sent from the Mathematics and Naval School to every provincial capital to serve as teachers. Forty-three "cipher schools" were founded but only about twenty-three ever operated at any one time, and by 1725 sixteen had closed permanently. Only 300 students ever completed the course in Peter's reign. Discipline, hardly conducive to attendance let alone to enlightenment, was the order of the day: "Students shall endeavor to learn what their teachers teach, and they shall receive with complete attention all the lessons which said teachers shall teach them, and shall have proper respect for them under pain of punishment."

Ironically, the parish schools of the Church were far more successful and actually expanded their enrollments in the eighteenth century. When Peter compelled the creation of diocesan schools in the Spiritual Regulation of 1721, large numbers of the sons of clergy who were in "cipher schools" transferred to the new Church establishments, and fourteen "cipher schools" closed thereafter. The bulk of students who enrolled in the Church schools were laymen, and after Peter's death many state servants were prepared through these schools, which were controlled by very conservative clergy. Peter himself by the end of his reign had centered his attention on the upper technical schools in Petersburg and had left the provinces to the Church.

Peter was not completely ignorant of the reasons for the difficulties of his secular schools. The Russian language was as yet unprepared to be a tool for such projects and Peter was making attempts to reshape it. Decent teachers were not available, for the graduates of the Mathematics School in Petersburg were channeled largely to civil or military duties, and foreigners would not deign to learn Russian. Further, money was required but was constantly diverted to other projects which the Tsar considered of higher priority. At the same time, the nobility resisted the schools and employed bribery and feigned insanity to shield themselves; Peter's schools succeeded inversely with their distance from Petersburg. Lastly, Peter never intended to found an educational system dedicated to "popular enlightenment." He sought a training system for state servants and did not appreciate broader schemes until late in his reign. Peter may have listened to the advice of Leibniz so freely given to the Tsar: that it was easier to educate a people who knew nothing, whose collective mind was a *tabula rasa*, since there were then no innate obstacles to resist new learning. If so, then Peter and Leibniz themselves had much to learn; the collective Muscovite mind was hardly a *tabula rasa*, and teaching geometry to adults who could neither read nor write was a task worthy of a better mind than even that of Gottfried Wilhelm von Leibniz.

It was this general pattern of obstacles which encouraged Peter nearly in the last moments of his reign to consider the establishment of some general institution charged with the total educational development. The Tsar had already founded a Public Library and a Museum in Petersburg, but an educational memorandum from Leibniz in 1716 strongly urged Peter to adopt a comprehensive program in the form of an Academy of Sciences. Within the past fifty years such academies had been founded in France, Prussia, and England, and in 1717 the Tsar himself had been elected a member of the French Academy. The Imperial Academy of Sciences was founded in 1724 but did not really begin to operate until after the Tsar's death. Its charter was based on that of the Academy in Berlin and envisioned faculties in mathematics, physics, and the humanities. Although the history of the Academy belongs to another age, its charter was revealing of Peter's experiences with his own educational reforms. The charter explained that some states could afford a university for teaching young people and an academy dedicated to promoting science, but that Russia had different needs. An academy solely to patronize the sciences would have no effect on the Russian population and a teaching university alone would not survive since "there are no elementary schools or seminaries in which the young can learn fundamentals before they proceed to more advanced subjects." The Russian Academy would therefore serve three functions, usually separated, by "promoting and developing the sciences while at the same time . . . giving public instruction to a group of students . . . and instructing others so that they in turn may teach young people."

Peter's reply to the mining expert and amateur historian, Vasili Tatischev, is revealing of the Tsar's views of his educational experiments as well as of the Petrine reforms in general. Tatischev objected vigorously to the founding of an Academy because there were not sufficient scholars to support its work properly. The tiring Tsar, near the end of his work, replied:

> Suppose I am able to bring in great harvests, but there is no mill and there is no water in the area to run such a mill. But some distance off there is water, but no opportunity for me to build a canal for it because I cannot expect such a long life. Therefore I will build the mill and simply leave instructions that a canal is to be dug; this will force my successors to provide the water for the mill which I have already built.

※ 8 ※

Saint Petersburg,
Opposition, and Support

The most spectacular architectural achievement of the eighteenth century, the city of Saint Petersburg, was raised up out of the mud to glorify the achievements of Peter and to give his secular state a mortal home. Not even the Sun King had raised up a city at his command, for Versailles was no new Paris. This was the planned city of the age, created where no city would otherwise have been, populated by citizens who did not choose to dwell there, enriched by a reluctant commerce, governed by a bureaucracy which condemned it as a prison. Yet it was also the city which glorified the great lords of the new era who had had no rank in Moscow, which launched the ships no Muscovite had ever sailed, which housed in pastel palaces the new offices of an imperial administration of which Muscovy had never dreamed, which welcomed and nurtured the European cultural life which Moscow had despised. Truly Saint Petersburg was the microcosm of Peter's achievements and of his failures and was the emotional symbol of the opposition to his work and the support which it engendered.

The city of Saint Petersburg was founded in May, 1703, when Peter put down the crude foundations of the Peter and Paul Fortress at the Neva's mouth. It was founded in the darkest days of the Swedish War and for six years the energy invested in its expansion was a gamble wagered by the struggling Tsar against the Swedish King. Peter won his gamble at Poltava, and, as he himself happily proclaimed, "the final stone in the foundation of Petersburg has been laid." The city was not named for the Tsar himself, despite history's insistence that it be so; it was named for Peter's patron saint, the Apostle Peter. But if the city had a respectable Orthodox saint for its patron, it was significant that the saint's name took a Dutch form.

Petersburg was set down upon a most desolate spot, whose atmosphere was recreated by Alexander Pushkin in "The Bronze Horseman":

> The moss-grown miry banks with rare
> Hovels were dotted here and there
> Where wretched Finns for shelter crowded;
> The murmuring woodlands had no share
> Of sunshine, all in mists beshrouded.[1]

It would cost much to build this city—much in treasure, much in lives, and much in national morale. Peter wanted this city badly. He wanted to be far from the Muscovite boyars and the Orthodox establishment who used Moscow as some ancient spiritual shield against the will of the Tsar. He wanted a city which was neither a Third Rome nor a New Jerusalem symbolizing past spiritual greatness, but another bustling Amsterdam as a sign of present power and achievements yet to be. Petersburg would also be his guarantee against the Swedes. There would be no border wars here again; those who would wrest the Baltic coast from Russia must henceforth bring down the state. Nor was Peter unmindful of the rivalry with the newly conquered Baltic ports of Riga and Revel which drained the hinterlands of Poland; Russia must have its own port, its own pride, its own proper tabernacle for its new government. Petersburg was declared the capital in 1715, and the offices of government moved reluctantly but surely to its timbered quays.

The decision that Petersburg was necessary to Muscovy was easy to make; to build the city was a bit more difficult. Compulsion was required on a vast scale, and labor conscripts had to be gathered from all over Muscovy to carry dirt in baskets for mile upon mile to fill in the swampy bottoms before any building could even be begun. The late nineteenth-century Russian historian Vasili Klieuchevsky called the city "a mass grave," the early-nineteenth-century intellectual Nikolai Karamzin thought it "built on tears and corpses," but Tsar Peter called it "my Paradise." Visitors to modern Leningrad would not recognize Peter's city in its core; the glory of this most charming

---

[1] Alexander Pushkin, "The Bronze Horseman," in John Cournos, ed., *A Treasury of Russian Life and Humor* (New York, Coward-McCann, Inc., 1943), p. 115. Reprinted by permission of Edward Arnold (Publishers) Ltd.

of European cities still lay ahead in the century. In the years before Poltava rough houses were scattered about half-built, and the swamps swallowed lumber, stone, and bodies. Petersburg in those days seemed no more than a frontier settlement on the periphery of some distant empire. Peter spent much time in his city, personally following the work of Menshikov, who was entrusted with its fate. While Menshikov labored on his grandiose palace on the Vasilievsky Island, Peter was content in his tiny two-room cottage on the Neva's Moscow side. He wrote once from the flooded town with the amazing optimism that comforted him always: "The day before yesterday a west-southwest wind blew up such waters as they say have never been seen here before. They rose twenty-one inches from the floor of my house, and in the garden and across the street people were going about in boats. The waters remained for only three hours. I enjoyed watching how the people, the peasants and their wives, sat on the roofs and perched in the trees during the flood."

By the end of Peter's reign Saint Petersburg had expanded rapidly. A member of the Polish legation reported in 1720 that "the area has a city look about it already; there are houses, docks and enormous buildings with annexes and all the conveniences." The population had risen from those few ragged Finnish fishermen to over 100,000. The Fortress was nearly finished, the Admiralty was sending ships down its ways, an inn welcomed visitors, and palaces bearing the names of the new Petrine plutocrats were being completed: Apraksin, Gagarin, Menshikov, Buturlin, Shafirov, Yaghuzhinsky, Chernishev, and even Peter's sister, Natalia. The flooding Neva was being slowly contained by timbered quays, the rudiments of a harbor welcomed ships from many parts of Europe, and the Summer Gardens already reminded visitors of more famous European parks. The Nevski Prospekt was as yet but a post road to the Nevski Monastery, but the streets of the town were hung with lanterns, night patrols passed among them in protection against brigands, and boats plied from the mainland to the islands in place of bridges yet to come. By 1725 the contrast of Pushkin aptly applied:

> Where once, by this low-lying shore,
> In waters never known before
> The Finnish fisherman, sole creature,
> And left forlorn by step-dame Nature,
> Cast ragged nets—today, along
> These shores, astir with life and motion,

Vast shapely palaces in throng
And towers are seen: from every ocean
From the world's end, the ships come fast,
To reach the loaded quays at last.[2]

But Petersburg, thrive though it might, was a microcosm of the Russia over which it presided and thus a focus of the complaints against the programs which were wrought there in the name of this new Russia. If ever the secular absolute state had an incarnation, it was in this city which it had given birth. How valid the reflection of the twentieth-century Russian novelist Andrey Biely in his novel which bears the city's name: "Call it Saint Petersburg, or Peter (it is all one)."

To the general population of Muscovy, Saint Petersburg was a distant but ever-intruding menace. To the peasant it was the city of army conscription and forced labor, the city from which came the orders that tore him from his land for interminable military duty or mutilation or death, or that transported him to unknown places to dredge a harbor or dig a canal, or that planted him, unwilling and unhappy, in some mine or foundry far from home. To all of them it was the city of taxes, rearing its foreign grandeur on the backs of the people. Nor was it simply a city of burdens to the peasant, but an unholy city into which neither he nor his parish priest in their beards and Muscovite clothing could or wished to enter. The records of the police inquiries in the Preobrazhensky office were endless lists of peasant outcries: "Since God has sent him to be Tsar, we have no happy days; the village is weighted down with sending rubles and half-rubles, and horses, and carts, and there is no rest." From the women came the lament that "he has carried off our husbands to be soldiers and left us and our children orphans to pass our lives in weeping." It was all summarized in the faceless cry of an anguished people: "Bloodsucker! He has eaten up the world!"

To the craftsmen of the towns Petersburg was the city of the bureaucrat who might tax them to their deaths or transfer them to some distant state project, and the city of the persecutor who would forcibly inquire into the state of their faith. To the merchant it was the city of enforced commerce toward which he unwillingly bent his steps from the comfortable road to Archangel and in which he saw consumed in costs the profits of his labor. To the Cossacks of the steppes and to the

[2] *Ibid.*

native peoples of the Ural frontier, the Tatars and the Bashkirs, it was the imperial city of a foreign power which stole their freedom, conscripted their sons, forced their conversions, and leveled them all to the ranks of Muscovite slaves.

The bulk of the hierarchy of the Russian Orthodox Church saw Petersburg as the city of the Synod, the city of the Ukrainian clergy who lorded it over the ministers of the ancient faith, the living sign of their degradation and of their "headless condition," and an impious reproach to the holy city of Moscow. To the run of the parish clergy, Petersburg was closer to an evil city where Roman Catholics and Protestants built their churches with impunity and perpetrated their ugly rituals to subvert the true believers. To the Old Believers and their myriad sympathizers, Petersburg was the earthly abode of the Antichrist, the capital of materialism, the physical manifestation of the triumph of evil in the world where Peter's second and foreign wife wallowed in debauchery and shame. "Therefore," said a schismatic tract from the Solovietsky Monastery, "he has taken craftily to himself not only the power of the Tsar but also the authority of God, and claiming to be an autocratic pastor, a headless head over all the opponents of Christ, Antichrist. Wherefore we must conceal ourselves in the deserts, just as the Prophet Jeremiah ordered the children of God to flee from Babylon."

This span of popular discontent which focused on the "New Babylon" was manifested in sullen stubbornness or dark despair on the part of most, and the urge to escape or to strike out in revolt for many more. The central provinces were hardest hit by desertions as the runaways headed for the northern provinces, the southern Cossack lands, or for Siberia. As has been mentioned, Peter's campaigns into the steppes helped to close several large holes through which his beleaguered peasantry had slipped to freer lands. The Tsar's decree against peasant flights was issued in 1707, demanding that "these fugitives and peasants, with their wives, children, and belongings, should be returned to their previous landlords from whom they fled within six months of this decree." Still, the government acknowledged 200,000 cases of runaways from 1719 to 1726.

For others flight was but the prelude to active resistance. As were the reigns of his father and grandfather, Peter's reign too was rife with popular revolts. The rebellions of the *streltsi* even before 1700 have already been described. It was, however, the southeastern frontier which was the traditional incubator of revolt, and it was in Astrakhan, to which many of the *streltsi* had been exiled, where wild rumors about the Tsar and his plans were magnified. Here the taxes on beards and clothes were resisted, taxes in general were denounced, and, in something of a peasant parody of the Petrine reform, the rumor was spread that the Tsar intended to marry all the young people of the city to foreigners. Merchants from many parts of the country who were on business in Astrakhan joined the agitation, which was well stocked with Old Believer propositions. In 1705 the entire area broke into open revolt. General Sheremetiev, leading the army against the Astrakhan rebels, complained that he had "never seen such a crazy rabble; they are bloated with malice and with the belief that we are fallen from Orthodoxy." The revolt, which lasted nearly a year, ended with bloody executions and many exiles.

No sooner had the lower Volga been pacified, with the Tsar's secret thanks to God that the Yaik and Don Cossacks had not been aroused at the same time, when the eastern frontier rose in rebellion. The Bashkirs, resentful of taxes and conscriptions, marched into the valley of the Volga in 1708 and for more than a year ravaged the lands of Russian settlers and approached even to the gates of Kazan. More than 300 villages were destroyed in their rampage before they were routed in turn, and the smoke that hung over the valley of the Volga was a misty omen of the revolts still to come in that century. Russia was already suffering the serious spasms of Empire.

Nor did the Cossacks accept their new subservience without resistance. Because they had not followed the Hetman Mazepa into the arms of the Protestant Swede did not mean that they were happy in the painful embrace of the Muscovite Tsar. In perennial hope of recovering their lost autonomy, the Cossacks had, as of old, continued to accept runaway Muscovites into their communities and to found new and better-fortified towns in the steppe. Prince Dolguruki was sent by Peter into the valley of the Don in 1707 to enforce the orders forbidding these practices, and one of the Don Cossack hetmen, Kondraty Bulavin, ambushed him on the way and massacred his entire contingent. Bulavin then fled to the Zaporozhian, or Dnieper, Cossacks and returned to the Don region with large bands of rebels. His decrees hailed the heritage of the brigand-hero of the seventeenth century, Stenka Razin, and his rebellion proclaimed "the defense of the house of God's Holy Mother and the Orthodox Church against the infidel and Greek teachings which the boyars and the Germans wish to impose upon us." To his banner came Cossacks, peasants, Old

Believers, and labor conscripts from the Voronezh district. By the middle of 1708 the revolt had grown so as to threaten the central provinces, and even regular troops in the Azov district and elsewhere had begun to desert to join the cause. Ultimately, the weight of Peter's trained and equipped armies crushed the revolt and Bulavin committed suicide to evade capture, but the remnants of the revolt smouldered for many years.

The popular revolts, which mingled the varied frustrations of peasantry, Old Believers, Cossacks, nationalities, and industrial laborers, were all fearsome to Tsar Peter. Both the Bashkir and Bulavin revolts, for example, took place as Charles XII was making his way toward an invasion of Muscovy and certainly influenced his decision to attack at the time and in the place that he did. In perspective, however, these revolts were still in the style of the seventeenth century—passionate, violent, terror-ridden, sweeping like wildfire across the grassy steppe—but unorganized, programless, and deeply wracked by internal dissensions and jealousies. What did the rebels of the Don and the Volga want? They sought a just, lawful, and Orthodox Tsar, an all-loving father who would destroy the infamous landlords and tame the rampaging bureaucrats, repudiate foreignisms and restore and honor the old ways, strike down the burdensome taxes, the death-dealing conscriptions, and the enslaving industrial establishments. They wished, in short, to roll back the "modern" world which was bearing down on them, and in this aspiration they had a more monumental force to resist than simply the perverse will of an evil Tsar. Sympathy surely goes out to those who joined unequal battle with the modern state in the process of its formation, but the weight of history was with the "Antichrist."

These popular forces fighting the rearguard action of a dying age were not really the strongest opposition which threatened the work of the dynamic Tsar. Far more dangerous than the powerless masses seeking to avoid suffering were the powerful elites seeking to continue their power. The remnants of the old Moscow nobility, immersed now in the new *generalitet*, or higher ranks of the state service, at least shared the longing for old times which characterized the popular revolts. In those golden times before the Table of Ranks, the ancient families of Moscow had marked out the government of Muscovy as their exclusive preserve. Now the lowly provincials sat beside them or even above them in offices of state and, even worse, the efficient German barons of the conquered Baltic provinces with their training and their tradition were now flocking to service posts in Petersburg. For the old metropolitan nobility then, Saint Petersburg was the city of the "fledglings" and the "accidental men" who merited none of the power and preference lavished upon them by the Tsar, the city of the infamous Table of Ranks which lifted the lowly over the heads of the deserving, the city of the foreigners, of high prices and enforced building of new palaces, of miserable living conditions far from their cherished estates in the environs of Moscow. Petersburg was to them a premeditated assault on Moscow and all that it had meant to these ancient service families. Revealing is the testimony of Prince Kropotkin, an aristocrat of the nineteenth century, who reminisced about his youth:

> Some fifty years ago there lived in this quarter [the Old Equerries' Quarter] and slowly died out, the old Moscow nobility, whose names were so frequently mentioned in the pages of Russian history before the times of Peter I, but who subsequently disappeared to make room for the newcomers, "the men of all ranks" called into service by the founder of the Russian state. Feeling themselves supplanted at the Saint Petersburg court, these nobles of the old stock retired either to the Old Equerries Quarter in Moscow, or to their picturesque estates in the country round about the capital, and they looked with a sort of contempt and secret jealousy upon the motley crowd of families which came "from no one knew where" to take possession of the highest functions of the government, in the new capital on the banks of the Neva.[3]

But these families struggled before they retired, as Kropotkin indicates, to nurse their contempt at the end of the century. The old Moscow service families were dangerous to Peter in his day and after, precisely because they had enjoyed and still enjoyed a measure of power, and because they were, in such persons as Dmitri Golitsin and Prince Kurakin, cultivated, thoughtful, and patriotic men. They were neither ignorant, reactionary, violently superstitious, nor irrational in their attachment to Muscovite custom; but they were conservative and traditionalist, and were convinced that the flood of crude, ignorant, inexperienced, and dangerously ambitious provincials into positions of power threatened the stability of the state and the sensible continuity of its growth. They disapproved also of the personal life of the Tsar, his carousing with foreigners, his divorce and

[3] James Allen Rogers, ed., *Peter Kropotkin's Memoirs of a Revolutionist* (Garden City, N.Y.: Doubleday & Company, Inc., 1962), p. 2.

remarriage to a camp follower, not out of some passionate reaction against the Antichrist but for the simple civic reason that it demeaned the office of Tsar and undermined the authority of the state it represented. These Moscow nobles shared the same intimate mixture of idealism and personal ambition as do most politicians, and they easily confused their own political fortunes with the welfare of the state. Their hope for the restoration of stable Muscovite government and the rededication of the Muscovite Tsardom, and their hope for their own political restoration at the same time, was Peter's son, the Tsarevich Alexei.

What the metropolitan nobility hoped of the heir to the throne was exposed (if we may jump ahead of our story for a moment) by young Alexei's mistress at his later trial. She revealed, with an abandon which spoke for her veracity, the hopes and expectations which orbited around the person of the Tsarevich; her testimony constituted a political program of the old families. They were, for example, depending on Alexei for the abandonment of Saint Petersburg, not because it was an unholy city but because it was ridiculously situated, incredibly expensive, and separated from the main stream of Muscovite life; it simply did not hold the people's allegiance as did Moscow, and the state needed allegiance in these days far more than it needed coercion. Gregory Dolguruki, of most prestigious family, wrote to a friend in 1717 that "although provincial governors have a hard life (and where can one be now without trouble?) still I think that none of them would leave his province and be willing to come and live here in Petersburg." The Tsar's half-sister, whose heart was with the old families, uttered the malediction which lasted longest in memory over the city: "Petersburg will not last beyond our time. Let it be a desert!"

The old noble families also stood firmly against the prosecution of the Great Northern War and wished to retire within the old borders to restore order and tend to the public welfare, which was being sadly neglected. They were in a real sense "isolationist," arguing that the rulers of former times conquered for the salvation of the state but that Tsar Peter conquered in avarice; thus his conquests only promised ever deeper involvement with the other states of Europe and ever-recurring war. The conquests of former times had provided benefits in lands to the nobility and taxes to the state, but the new territories brought only expenses for their conquest and defense and the promise of constant friction with great powers which would permanently prevent the government from attending to the great internal problems of the realm. Worse, the new conquests were bringing Baltic German landlords into Russian service to "dance on our heads." What enemy could wreak the damage to Muscovy which the Tsar's wars had done?

The metropolitan nobles stood also for the abandonment of the Tsar's beloved navy. From whom was there danger from the sea, they asked, that Muscovy should expend so much treasure to defend against? The Swedes were the only northern power who could come to the attack over the water, and if the silly outpost at Petersburg was abandoned they would make no headway after Poltava in an invasion of the central provinces. On the Black Sea frontier the Turks were now busy setting their house in order, as every state should. And against what other European power would Muscovy be foolish enough to launch a naval attack? Every people had its native skills, and it would be foolhardy to attempt to rival the English or the Dutch command of the sea. Therefore, they reasoned, let the vast expenses of a navy be abandoned, and let visions of a native merchant marine be similarly dismissed, since the foreigners handled the carrying trade efficiently enough and Muscovy benefited from the extremely favorable balance of trade.

Finally, the old families considered themselves badly treated in the new dispensation, which treatment in turn reflected badly on the public welfare and the economic well-being of the state. Service in distant Petersburg or in other parts of Europe dragged them from their estates in Moscow province where they had been accustomed to administer their lands personally and, one must say in fairness, efficiently, while they performed their service. An official government report of the eighteenth century described Moscow as "composed of many houses of the nobility that by their plan, spaciousness, and the great number of servants, constituted, rather than city establishments, whole villages where lived a self-contained population of commoners of various conditions and trades." The nobles, proud of their patrimony, now watched mournfully from Petersburg as those estates fell into disrepair and their incomes drained away into the high costs of life in the capital. Surely a prosperous and dedicated group of hereditary administrators was more beneficial to the state than a motley horde of ignorant clerks whose lands went wasting.

These noble families, then, posed threats to the most cherished projects of the Tsar: the Baltic provinces, Saint Petersburg, the navy, and the new service nobility. They were, in all, unhappy with the necessary consequences of the transformation of provincial Muscovy into the vast Russian Empire. It was not the first time, and surely not the last, that honest and dedicated men would balk at the convulsions caused in a society by the "modernization" of the state; these nobles shared something of the reluctance of the peasants below them to pay the inevitable price of power. But they were good state servants in a respected Muscovite tradition; they planned no revolts and threatened no violence which would destroy far more than they would build. As with all good civil servants, they abhorred civil strife in themselves as in others. Their hopes for the future and faith in past techniques sought legal and traditional outlets; this hope and this faith was vested for a time in Alexei, the heir to the throne.

Peter had to bear the traditional monarch's cross, the problem of succession. Even Machiavelli wrote as if the prince were immortal, offering no hint of advice as to how the continuity of the prince's work was to be guaranteed. Peter knew, as his conversations often indicated, that his work was spasmodic and unfinished and would require the attention of his dynasty to revise and to complete. Peter found this problem of continuity difficult to resolve, and indeed he did not solve it. He was not alone in his troubles, for his generation was one of crises of succession across Europe, most notably in England, France, Spain, and Prussia. The Tsar could order the creation of a city but no order in the world could compel the creation of a human being to fit the future's needs. The Tsarevich Alexei was an immense disappointment to his father, and ultimately, because of the focus he provided for those who would roll back the reforms, a threat to the Petrine establishment.

Alexei had been born within the first year of his father's marriage, in 1690, and had been taken from his mother to be raised by relatives when Eudoxia was implicated in the *streltsi* revolts of 1698 and forced into a convent. The Tsarevich began at an early age to resent his father's treatment of his mother. Peter, as part of his dynastic maneuvering after Poltava, ordered Alexei to marry Charlotte von Wolfenbuettel, sister-in-law of the next Austrian Emperor. The marriage took place in 1711 and was most unhappy; it ended quickly when Charlotte died in childbirth. Alexei was extremely religious, or perhaps pietistic is a better word. He was usually malingering with some disease or other, drank heavily and showed it, and demonstrated no particular aptitude for either military or civil service; he was his father's son in neither physique nor character and a classic case of alienation rapidly set in between the Tsar and heir. Alexei told his chaplain in confession of his wish to see his father dead, to which the priest replied: "God will forgive; we have all desired his death, for the burdens borne by the people are great."

Part of the antipathy between father and son was bound up with Peter's remarriage. Catherine Skavronsky was a Latvian prisoner of war taken at Marienburg in the Livonian campaign of 1702; she passed from hand to hand until she came under the benign care of Alexander Menshikov. It was in Menshikov's house in 1703 that the Tsar met this buxom, crude, rather ignorant but happy and hard-living foreigner. In 1712, despite the clerical and popular outcry against a remarriage, and to a foreigner, Peter made Catherine his wife. Their relationship was a stable and happy one until the last few stormy years; Catherine bore the Tsar eleven children although most died in infancy, and even accompanied him on campaigns. Peter's letters to his wife were those of a happy and home-loving husband; in late 1709, for example, he wrote from Warsaw:

> Little Mother, thanks for your package. I send you some fresh lemons. You surely joke about our amusements here, we have none, for we are old and not that kind of person. . . . Give my regards to Auntie. Her bridegroom had an interview the day before yesterday with Ivashka [he drank too much—Ed.] and fell on the boat and is now powerless; break the news gently to Auntie so she doesn't go to pieces.

Catherine was commissioned to produce an alternative heir to the repugnant Alexei, and in October of 1715 she gave birth to a son, Peter (who died in infancy) at the same time that Alexei gave the Tsar a grandson, also named Peter. The Tsar seized his opportunity provided by the choice of heirs to warn the Tsarevich to mend his ways and bend to the Tsar's will and become a devoted son and pupil, or face disinheritance. In September, 1716, the impatient Tsar wrote to Alexei:

> My Son: . . . When I bade you goodbye and asked you about your resolution in a certain matter, you consistently replied in the same way: that because of your feebleness you were not fit for the inheritance and wished rather to go into a monastery. Then I told you to think this over seriously and to communicate to me what resolution

you had taken. I have waited seven months for your reply. . . .
Therefore now . . . immediately make a resolution for the first or the
second. . . . I must make sure that this is finally concluded, for I see
you are wasting your time in your usual idleness.

Alexei, fearful of losing his peasant mistress and spending his life
immured in a monastery and even more fearful of the violent wrath
of his father, fled to Vienna. His brother-in-law the Emperor was
terribly embarrassed by the presence of this political refugee, housed
him temporarily in the Tyrol, and then urged him to take up residence
in Naples. It was there that Peter Tolstoi, the Tsar's policeman, found
him and cajoled him into returning by promising him the Tsar's
clemency and reconciliation. Tolstoi delivered a letter from Peter to
Alexei. "You have run away and put yourself under foreign protection like a traitor. . . . I therefore send this last message to you so
that you may obey my will as M. Tolstoi and M. Rumiantsev will
convey it to you. If you submit to me, I guarantee and promise by
God and His Judgment that you will not be punished and that I will
show you my best love." Alexei, never strong-willed, accepted the
terms his father had no intention of keeping and came home. In
1718, after extensive examination of the Tsarevich under torture in
the Preobrazhensky Office, it was announced in a circular to foreign
governments that the Tsarevich had "died in the moment of heavy
judgment on his crimes from a cruel malady quite similar to an attack of apoplexy. He confessed freely all his crimes." Peter had, in
any honest evaluation, killed his son. But while the Tsar might bury
the body of the Tsarevich, he could not bury the aristocratic resentments which had gathered around him; those resentments could only
be intensified by the violence of the Tsar against even his own
family.

The resistance of the old Moscow families would return again before
Peter was long in his tomb and before they themselves faded into the
amalgamated Russian aristocracy of the later century. Rather than a
sympathetic heir upon whom to lean, they would have the chaos of
a disputed succession within which to win their way. One of the most
unpleasant pieces of the Petrine heritage was the contested succession.
The tortuous windings of that succession are not our affair here, but
the death of Alexei did leave behind a condition which clearly
weakened the autocratic power in the years ahead. There were, when
Peter died in 1725, three lines of Romanov succession and no succes-

sion law except the monarch's choice. Before the eighteenth century had ended, rulers of all three lines would reign and be overthrown.

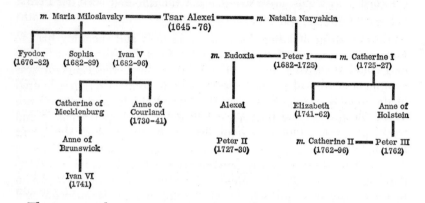

There was, then, vast opposition to the reforming Tsar, rolling through the frontier outposts of the Old Belief and the frustrated Cossack councils, measured in the moaning of a beleaguered peasantry and in the reasoned complaints of the merchantry and the old noble families, and mounting, in the person of the Tsarevich, to the steps of the throne. Historians have made much of that opposition, and well they should. The creation of the secular absolute state created terror and resentment wherever it was undertaken, and the fury of that resentment was a common European phenomenon in the early modern age. Leaderless, unorganized, and ineffectual though such opposition was, it served at least to remind monarchs that men were never so easy to manipulate as administrative charts. But one hopes that the wise reader has nursed a question in the process of examining the annals of opposition. If the story ends here, then how did any piece or parcel of those reforms survive? For as the reader knows, survive they did. Clearly, forces were at work to shore up and save the essential core of the reforms, and those forces must have been strong enough to maintain the reforms until, within a few generations even the opposition faded or grew enough accustomed to them to claim them as a national heritage.

The most obvious group working for the preservation of Peter's reforms was the body of "fledglings," or "accidental persons," who owed their rise and fortunes to the friendship of the Tsar and whose very lives were bound up with the future of his institutions. They numbered among them the great *verkhovniki,* or supreme lords of the realm: Catherine I, crowned Empress by Peter in 1724; Alexander Menshikov, the German Ostermann who directed foreign affairs; General Munnich; and others. How long, for example, could Catherine Skavronsky, this foreign camp follower who was no Empress in Muscovite eyes, expect to survive a conservative reaction? Or how long could Menshikov survive the attacks of the jealous aristocrats he had superseded with such arrogance? Indeed, how long would any of the foreigners keep their places if an anti-foreign reaction set in? These "fledglings" had been placed in positions of power by Peter's work, and any failure to defend that work would be political and personal suicide.

In similar straits were the "westernized" nobility among the great families, men such as Peter Tolstoi and Michael Dolguruki, who had forsaken the cause of their fathers, brothers, and cousins of the old nobility to give willing service in the Petrine order. Some had done so for idealism, some for profit; most for both. They had risen high, in many cases higher than their forefathers in Muscovite service, but they earned enmity on the way. Peter Tolstoi, for example, the betrayer of the Tsarevich, could hardly expect pleasant treatment from a government formed of Alexei's adherents.

The commitment of the Petrine favorites was given theoretical framework by the ecclesiastical and political propagandist Theofan Prokopovich, who had as much to lose from a post-Petrine reaction as any of the others. Was he not an infected clergyman of Ukraine responsible for the headless condition of the Church and the Protestant subversion of Orthodoxy? Prokopovich authored, at Peter's invitation, an essay entitled *Justice is the Monarch's Will,* which provided foundations for Petrine practice. Here and in many sermons and tracts Prokopovich insisted on the Hobbesian nature of man, steeped in anarchy and destruction, which demanded an all-powerful Tsar to establish peace and order in society. Prokopovich's works judiciously mixed scriptural precedents, concepts of natural law, and Russian historical experience. One of his sermons, for example, a "Sermon on Royal Authority and Honor," had a revealing subtitle: "How It Is Established in the World by God Himself, and How Men Are Obliged to Honor Kings and Obey Them, and Who the People Are Who Oppose Them and How Great Is the Sin They Have." It was no accident that the sermon was delivered in the midst of the affair of the Tsarevich. Without the autocrat, said Prokopovich in words which conjure up the *Leviathan,*

> . . . there is tumult and quaking in the country, bloody private quarrels among the great, but among the small men of good conscience wailing, weeping, affliction, while evil men like fierce beasts loosed from their bonds, attack in waves everywhere, murdering and plundering. . . . Is not Russia herself witness enough? For I think that she will not soon forget what she suffered after the misdeeds of Gudunov and how close she was to final destruction.[4]

But the strongest bulwark of the Petrine reforms by the end of the reign was, irony of ironies, the provincial nobility. How vigorously they had resisted enforced service, education, travel, preferment, political power, and the new manners! Yet, only twenty years in the new world of society and politics and how rapidly the sons deserted the ways of the fathers. Having tasted the joys of city life, caroused in the Guards, traveled in Paris or London, acquired a taste for fine living, and enjoyed the financial grants of their ruler, who among these noble sons would choose to return to the mud-hut villages of the provinces to take up their hoes and plows again? These provincial nobles still resisted many of the irritating aspects of service and would continue to seek their amelioration, but the Table of Ranks was dear to them, insuring their right to sit beside and even above the ancient service families and ultimately forming both into a unified aristocracy. The Petrine academies were useful to them, guaranteeing them preferment to match the bloodlines of their jealous urban rivals. The Guards Regiments were their especial enclaves, promising them income and prestige and power which they would defend with vigor in the turbulent century to come. The new "men of all ranks," therefore, might balk at the permanent service imposed upon them and set out to reshape the reforms more to their liking, but the truth was that Peter had done his work well. The service nobility became a force of its own, controlling the offices of state and the command of the army and the Guards and resolved not to yield their gains to the partisans of the past.

The Petrine reform had thus created its most vigorous support in the new nobility. There was, of course, a price to be paid for that

---

[4] Feofan Prokopovich, "Sermon on Royal Authority and Honor," in Marc Raeff, ed., *Russian Intellectual History: An Anthology* (New York: Harcourt, Brace & World, Inc., 1966), p. 29.

support and the price was paid many times over in the century ahead. All that these nobles asked for their continued support of the autocratic power and the bureaucratic state was guaranteed freedom to dominate their lands and serfs without government interference. That was a simple request which the Petrine government had already honored for its own purposes, but it was truly an immense price. Petrine government placed a severe limit upon its successors in finding the means to prolong its life; it surrendered direct control of the lives of the bulk of its subjects. The word "autocratic" then needs clear definition in the centuries after Peter's reign, and its practitioners had a healthy task before them to restore the ancient role of autocracy, before the people themselves lost faith in its ultimate efficacy.

✵ 9 ✵

The Petrine Testament

Peter died in 1725 and the manner of his death was wholly consistent with the manner of his life. Suffering from a painful kidney disease, he had plunged into the sea to help rescue some of his sailors and thereby aggravated the fever which ultimately brought him to his end. When he struggled to name his successor under the system of nomination which he himself had devised, in his weakness he could write only "leave all to . . ." before his hand slid from the page. That act dramatized one of the most serious shortcomings of his testament, for the success of the Petrine autocracy depended heavily on the quality of the person who exercised it and on his security in office and confidence in his authority. Peter left behind a more organized autocracy but also the weakness of a questionable succession, and the Tsar who had never accepted any limitation on his power to influence the present was as powerless in his last moments as any other man to determine the future.

Peter was only fifty-three years old when he died, still a relatively young man even in this age; Louis XIV of France had died at seventy-seven and Frederick William of Brandenburg at sixty-eight. But despite his age few Russians at the end of his reign could recall any ruler except Peter the Great; he had been officially on the throne for forty-three years. His reign might have been outstripped by Louis XIV's seventy-two years and matched by the Great Elector's forty-eight, but it was still substantial. Such a simple matter as the length of Peter's effective rule, and he was effective to the last month of his reign, was vitally important to the Petrine testament, for many of the reforms which were resisted in their origins had become so deeply rooted in the quarter century after 1700 that few of his enemies could really think of destroying them outright. There is a signal advantage in holding power long enough to convince your subjects that already at your death your work is a historical legacy. Franklin D. Roosevelt's four terms in the presidency of a modern republic certainly had some such effect.

There was little mourning at Peter's passing. In fact his death elicited much the same popular response as that of the Sun King— general rejoicing that the heavy burdens had at last been lifted from the shoulders of the lowly. The few who seemed to mourn his passing were actually mourning for themselves. These were the Petrine favorites, the scavengers who had pillaged and prospered beneath the protection of the eagle's wings; to them the future without their Emperor was a threat and they scuttled hurriedly, even around the deathbed of their leader, to insure continuing control of the machinery of state in the hands of their comrades, Menshikov and Catherine I. Perhaps, in the last years, most certainly in the last hours, Peter must have come to recognize that, of all his talents, judgment of people was the least developed. Among those "friends" who viewed the passing of the Emperor as politically inconvenient, none was even vaguely shaped in the Petrine mold.

Yet Peter left a legend behind him. Even those contemporaries who scorned his work and cheered his passing were in awe of his image, and the Petrine legend emerged in lively form within twenty years of the Emperor's death. The speed of the legend's formation was accelerated by comparison of the Tsar with his weak and colorless successors—Catherine I, Peter II, Anne, and the infant Ivan VI— beside whom Peter seemed an astonishing colossus. Violent and ruthless though he might have been, he at least had an obvious pride in his state, a willingness to work harder than the meanest of his laborers, an honesty unmatched by any bureaucrat, a character unimpressed by pomp, and a martial aura shared by none of his early successors. How rapidly the excesses of the Tsar-Reformer were forgotten, and how quickly in a generation of foreign politicians feeding at the Russian trough did Peter become a "true Russian"! Not until the apotheosis of Napoleon did another European state produce such a full-blown legend in so short a time.

By the middle of the century rulers in Russia were invoking that Petrine legend. His daughter Elizabeth came to the throne in 1741 in a coup which proudly exalted her ancestry and promised an end to the baneful influence of foreign princelings; as a matter of fact, Elizabeth's only real asset was her bloodline. And if his legend was soon a powerful force pressuring his successors and being invoked by all of them from Elizabeth and Catherine the Great onward, so his legend also became a European phenomenon. With Louis XIV and the Prussian princes he provided the practical lessons behind the theories of "enlightened despotism" which served to replace divine sanction as the rationale of absolutism; the legend of Peter sparked the imagination of the *lumières*. It was Feofan Prokopovich, delivering the Tsar's funeral oration, who set the outline of the Petrine legend: The Tsar was Russia's Samson, her Japhet, her Moses, Solomon, David, and Constantine.

> He has gone, but he has not left us poor and wretched; his enormous power and glory—manifested in the deeds I spoke of before—have remained with us. As he has shaped our Russia, so she will remain: he has made her lovable to good men, and she will be loved; he has made her fearful to her enemies, and she will be feared; he has glorified her throughout the world, and her glory will not end. He has left us spiritual, civil and military reforms. For if his perishable body has left us, his spirit remains.[1]

A curious quirk of the modern mind forces us to think of lies when we think of legends. But the Petrine legend was a strong reflection of truth. The Russian Empire at the end of Peter's reign was a great European power, and the clearer that fact became in the years between Poltava in 1709 and the annexation of the Crimea in 1783, the final partition of Poland in 1795, and the occupation of Paris in 1812, the larger loomed the figure of the Tsar who seemed so central to the development of that astonishing strength.

The emergence of Russia as a great European power seemed often to be treated by its western neighbors as some unique event, different in nature from the emergence of other European powers and thus requiring some specially tailored explanation. Such special explanations have often proceeded from ideas of the monolithic quality of "western civilization" and of the unique or even oriental quality of Russian civilization. It sometimes seems that these explanations were rooted in a western European ethnocentricity which considered it highly unlikely that a Slavic and Orthodox society could ever really

---

[1] Feofan Prokopovich, "Oration at the Funeral of Peter the Great," in Marc Raeff, ed., *Peter the Great: Reformer or Revolutionary?* (Boston: D. C. Heath and Company, 1963), p. 78.

raise itself by any inner resources to match arms and wits with the true tabernacles of civilization; surely such a Slavic society was colonial rather than European, representing one of the crude subject peoples of the world being painfully schooled at the altar of "western learning." The basis of such an imperialistic attitude toward Russian emergence is nicely caught by Alistair Cooke in a review of the memoirs of Harold Nicolson, when he describes that English statesman as "quietly convinced that outside the cultivated oases of England and France lay an encircling desert of rude and alien peoples." [2] From this perspective the rise of Russian power has always seemed some aberrant affront to the traditional wielders of world power, surely temporary and soon to be rolled back, an affront which requires some special explanation which includes a central role for the old powers in nurturing and guiding this poor primitive child.

It might lead us to a fairer view to recall that a succession of European states, of which Russia was but one, had attained great power at the dawn of the modern age. The middle of the seventeenth century, for example, had witnessed the emergence of two Muscovite neighbors, Denmark and Sweden, and no one has yet applied such terms as "europeanization" or "westernization" to such emergence. Nor did the process of great power development end with Russia; even when Peter's work was done, Prussia still had a long distance to travel to great power, and Italy even further. Peter can thus profitably be viewed as one of those northern monarchs of the seventeenth and early eighteenth centuries who presided over traditional societies in a state of drifting change which had the potential to achieve a large measure of influence in the general affairs of Europe; the attempt to realize that potential when undertaken was a substantial task requiring the elaboration of absolute governments and military institutions which in turn wrenched the societies which supported them and accelerated their changes in often unconscious but always vital ways.

The legacy of great power is, of course, a force all its own, at once liberating and limiting. Great power provided protection for Russia against exploitation by other states, which was the fate of Italy and Germany in the early modern era. England had feared such domination by Spain in the sixteenth century, and the Netherlands had responded in like manner to France in the seventeenth. The pursuit

[2] Alistair Cooke, "The Curious Vanity of a Latter-Day Pepys," *Life* (June 30, 1967), p. 6.

of great power thus had its rewards, and the freedom to work out a national destiny was chief among them. At the same time, great power status was one of the forces at work to preserve the Petrine reforms. One might have dreamed of destroying Petersburg, but would such an act be interpreted by the Swedes and others as a willingness to see the Baltic provinces and more reannexed? One might consider the Petrine navy a monstrosity, and indeed it suffered neglect in the years between Peter and Catherine II, but could it simply be scuttled in the face of the Turkish menace on the Black Sea and English presumption in the Baltic? One might think the autocracy an instrument of oppression over the nobility, but could the nobility afford the luxury of a Polish-style anarchy in a Europe of predatory states? One might even think serfdom a miserable evil, but could the Empire afford the internal disruption, the retreat into weakness which such a vast peasant reform would require?

The Great Power syndrome is thus a compelling one, and the Russian Empire was not the first or the last state to suffer its consequences. It would be fair to say that states into very recent times have considered their power and the protection of their international position as primary and the internal welfare of their citizens as secondary, or at least dependent on the former; the view that internal reform is the true key to international influence has been invoked only sporadically, powerful when it appears in revolutionary guise but usually quite temporary. Interpretations framed around the pursuit of great power, that Russian history is the story of a lagging society constantly struggling to bring itself abreast of its international role, have something to teach us. But we must recognize that such interpretations are not suited only to Russian experience and really apply to most major European powers; the same theme, for example, fits with equal utility the Revolutionary-Napoleonic era of French history.

The Petrine testament included not only the legend of Peter for his successors to contend with and the role of Great Power for them to protect, but included also the instrument of autocracy to implement their will. If Peter was effective in accomplishing the two primary tasks of his Romanov inheritance, then we must assume that he bequeathed these accomplishments to his successors. He completed the reconquest from the Time of Troubles and tamed his bellicose neighbors by installing Russia as a great power, and in the process he completed the recovery and restructuring of the absolutism which the Romanovs had espoused as the best means to insure outer protection and inner order. The autocracy was a strange part of the testament, for it was left behind as a legal instrument bound round with real limitations. I can recall asking students to evaluate a comment that "there is no such thing as an unlimited autocracy"; since that is obviously so, it is the form and extent of the limits that need our attention. Peter left the autocracy potentially limited by a larger and more articulated bureaucracy and really limited by the character of his successors, the factions upon whom weak rulers had to lean in order to survive on the throne, the necessity to cede to the interests of the nobility in order to preserve a legal freedom of action, and the requirement that to rule legally over all Russia it must deed away in practice the right to rule over the Russian peasantry.

These were serious limitations and meant that the autocracy would be seriously constrained in handling the difficult problems that were emerging in Russian society. Yet, inherent in the principle of autocracy was the means to do battle with its limitations and to change their form and character. The constant struggle to reshape the autocracy for modern duties was surely an arduous one, but the fact that it was never satisfactorily done does not mean that the struggle could not have been undertaken more often, more vigorously, and to better effect. I am not yet convinced, for example, that large-scale industrialization was impossible in autocratic and enserfed Russia and that only a Communist regime could bring it about. We can admit that the serf problem was amenable only to autocratic power, and that the emancipation of the serfs was undertaken primarily for reasons of state, to protect Russian power. We can admit that it was the weakness of autocracy which explains the failure of serf emancipation, and that the success of Stalinist absolutism in industrial transformation was a function of its completeness. But if we find that Peter was successful in adapting the seventeenth-century autocracy to the needs of his own age, we may still legitimately inquire how the leaders who seemed bound to maintain that autocracy contributed to its constant evolution as an effective instrument to serve the needs of state and society in their own eras. For example, the complaint against Catherine the Great as an "enlightened despot" might well be not that she was unenlightened but that she was no despot in any meaningful way. Several times in the history of the Russian Empire there were opportunities to emancipate the autocracy from some of its old rigidities and to unleash it against pressing problems. In these cases we must come to grips with the question of leadership. Petrine

Russia no more predestined such efforts to failure than seventeenth-century Muscovy predestined Peter to success.

It is clear from a consideration of the Petrine legend, the Great Power syndrome, and the autocracy, that the Russian Empire in 1725 was far different from the Muscovite Tsardom of 1682. An emerging autocratic state bent with indomitable will on military tasks had dragged a reluctant society into more modern forms, and had left that society in the throes of difficult adjustments. Russia had been more successful than most of its neighbors, thanks largely to its heritage and its leadership, in forging its absolutism and winning its military way; it was therefore plunged more deeply and more rapidly than many European states into the problems of a military secular state. Everywhere in Europe certain historical elements were emerging to define the age: nation-states were displacing dynastic agglomerations, bureaucracies were implementing the monarch's will in wider and more penetrating ways, industrial growth and international commerce were beginning to play havoc with guild forms and native handicrafts, colonial empires were being carved out by states with the means and the will, and secular learning and secular interests were threatening religious institutions and religious spirit. And, underlying all of these, the wars of the new monarchs were more general in extent and more crucial in their consequences to society than ever before. Petrine Russia leaped from the ranks of these movements to the van in one generation, and it is within this context of the shaping of early modern Europe that Russian achievements and Russian problems are best understood. If we may be permitted to repeat an earlier observation, it was those kingdoms that made the most intensive war for the longest time with some degree of success in this age which laid many of the foundations of the modern world; not least among such kingdoms was Petrine Russia.

Suggested Reading

The general European background of Peter's reign can be examined in the fine work of M. S. Anderson, *Europe in the Eighteenth Century* (New York, 1961); of John Wolf, *The Emergence of the Great Powers 1685-1715* (New York, 1951);* and of Penfield Roberts, *The Quest for Security 1715-1740* (New York, 1947).* The reader will find an encyclopedic coverage of Russian history in general and of Peter's reign in particular in the classic two volumes of Michael Florinsky, *Russia: A History and an Interpretation* (New York, 1953). A more recent work, possibly the finest concise history text in any field, is Nicholas Riasanovsky, *A History of Russia* (New York, 1963). An astonishing book which every reader will wish to have is James H. Billington, *The Icon and the Axe: An Interpretive History of Russian Culture* (New York, 1967).

The regency of Sophia is admirably examined in C. B. O'Brien, *Russia Under Two Tsars, 1682-1689* (Berkeley, 1952). A number of biographies of Peter are available in English, ranging from the eighteenth-century work of Voltaire to the nineteenth-century standards of Eugene Schuyler (1890) and Kasimir Waliszewski (1897). Recent biographies include those of Stephen Graham (New York, 1929), Constantin de Grunwald (New York, 1956), and Ian Grey (New York, 1960). The section on Peter from the general history of the great Russian historian Vasili Klyuchevsky is now available, *Peter the Great*, translated by Liliana Archibald (New York, 1963);* Klyuchevsky does not treat foreign affairs or cultural history. The

---

* Books marked with an asterisk are available in paperback.

most comprehensive short work on Peter, strong on biographical narrative and foreign policy, is B. H. Sumner, *Peter the Great and the Emergence of Russia* (New York, 1951);* Sumner has also provided us with the more specialized *Peter the Great and the Ottoman Empire* (Oxford, 1949). There is an extremely useful collection of contemporary and historical opinions on Peter provided in Marc Raeff, ed., *Peter the Great: Reformer or Revolutionary?* (Boston, 1963).*

Although this survey emphasizes works available in English, the reader with language abilities will benefit tremendously from the best recent work on Peter, R. Wittram, *Peter I, Czar und Kaiser: Zur Geschichte Peters des Grossen in Seiner Zeit*, 2 vols. (Göttingen, 1964), and from P. Miliukov, C. Seignobos, L. Eisenmann, *Histoire de Russie*, 3 volumes (Paris, 1932). Works of Russian historians available only in Russian include N. Ustryalov, *Istoriya tsarstvovaniya Petra Velikago*, 6 volumes (Saint Petersburg, 1858–63); S. Soloviev, *Istoriya Rossii s drevneishikh vremen* (Saint Petersburg, n.d.), Volume XVIII; and M. M. Bogoslavsky, *Petr I: Materialy dlia biografii*, 5 volumes (Leningrad, 1940–48). The papers of Tsar Peter began to appear before the Revolution, and their publication began again after World War II: *Pisma i bumagi imperatora Petra Velikago*, Volumes I–VII (Saint Petersburg, 1887–1918), Volumes VII–IX (1946–52). For a survey of the primary and secondary materials on Peter see the bibliographical section of V. I. Lebedev, B. D. Grekov, and S. V. Bakhrushin, eds., *Istoriya SSSR*, Volume I (Moscow, 1939).

Soviet interpretations of Petrine Russia are analyzed in Cyril E. Black, ed., *Rewriting Russian History* (New York, 1956),* and can be sampled in M. N. Pokrovsky, *History of Russia from Earliest Times to the Rise of Commercial Capitalism* (New York, 1928);* P. I. Lyashchenko, *History of the National Economy of the USSR to the 1917 Revolution* (New York, 1949); and John Letiche, ed. and trans., *A History of Russian Economic Thought* (Berkeley, 1964).

The appropriate sections of the following works are strongly recommended: M. S. Anderson, *Britain's Discovery of Russia 1553–1815* (London, 1958); Jerome Blum, *Lord and Peasant in Russia From the Ninth to the Nineteenth Century* (Princeton, 1961);* N. Hans, *History of Russian Educational Policy 1701–1917* (London, 1931); William E. Johnson, *Russia's Educational Heritage* (Pittsburgh, 1950); Walther Kirchner, *Commercial Relations Between Russia and Europe 1400–1800* (Bloomington, Indiana, 1966);* Anatole Mazour, *Modern Russian Historiography* (Princeton, 1958); Paul Miliukov,

Outlines of Russian Culture (New York, 1960),* with volumes on literature, religion, and art; D. S. Mirsky, *A History of Russian Literature* (New York, 1926);* Dmitri von Mohrenschildt, *Russia in the Intellectual Life of Eighteenth Century France* (New York, 1936); Marc Raeff, *The Origins of the Russian Intelligentsia* (New York, 1966);* Tamara Talbot Rice, *A History of Russian Art* (London, 1949);* Hans Rogger, *National Consciousness in Eighteenth Century Russia* (Cambridge, Mass., 1960); S. R. Tompkins, *The Russian Mind From Peter the Great Through the Enlightenment* (Norman, Oklahoma, 1953); S. V. Utechin, *Russian Political Thought* (New York, 1964);* Alexander Vucinich, *Science in Russian Culture: A History to 1860* (Stanford, 1963).

The following collections of articles contain discussions of relevant topics: Ivo J. Lederer, ed., *Russian Foreign Policy* (New Haven, 1962);* and Donald W. Treadgold, ed., *The Development of the USSR: An Exchange of Views* (Seattle, 1964).* Especially pertinent are the following articles reprinted in Sidney Harcave, ed., *Readings in Russian History,* Volume I (New York, 1962)*; George Vernadsky, "Serfdom in Russia"; Matthew Spinka, "Patriarch Nikon and the Subjection of the Russian Church to the State"; B. H. Sumner, "Peter the Great"; Max Beloff, "The Russian Nobility in the Eighteenth Century"; and Nadejda Gorodetsky, "Training for the Priesthood in Eighteenth Century Russia."

Collections of readings have grown in numbers, and the following have sections on this period composed of documents, contemporary accounts, and historical appraisals: Marthe Blinoff, ed., *Life and Thought in Old Russia* (University Park, Pennsylvania, 1961); Basil Dmytryshyn, ed., *Medieval Russia: A Source Book* and *Modern Russia: A Source Book* (New York, 1967);* Hans Kohn, ed., *The Mind of Modern Russia* (New York, 1962);* George Alexander Lensen, ed., *Russia's Eastward Expansion* (Englewood Cliffs, N. J., 1964);* L. Jay Oliva, ed., *Russia and the West from Peter to Khrushchev* (Boston, 1965);* Marc Raeff, ed., *Russian Intellectual History: An Anthology* (New York, 1966);* Warren B. Walsh, ed., *Readings in Russian History,* Volume I (Syracuse, 1963);* Alfred E. Senn, ed., *Readings in Russian Political and Diplomatic History,* Volume I (Homewood, Illinois, 1966);* and Ivar and Marion Spector, eds., *Readings in Russian History and Culture* (Boston, 1965).*

Contemporary accounts of Peter's reign are available in Peter Putnam, ed., *Seven Britons in Imperial Russia* (Princeton, 1952), and

Baron Korb, *Scenes from the Court of Peter the Great* (New York, 1921). Collections of literature include Leo Weiner, ed., *Anthology of Russian Literature* (New York, 1902–3), and the recent and invaluable Harold Siegel, ed., *The Literature of Eighteenth Century Russia*, 2 vols. (New York, 1967).* A fascinating Soviet historical novel is Alexei Tolstoi, *Peter the First* (New York, 1961).*

Index